D1253672

TEACHER AND CHILD

North Carolina Wesleyan College

WISDOM AND COURAGE THROUGH CHRISTIAN EDUCATION

1956

ROCKY MOUNT. N.C.

ALSO BY DR. HAIM G. GINOTT

Between Parent and Child
Between Parent and Teenager

Teacher and Child

A BOOK FOR PARENTS AND TEACHERS

Dr. HAIM G. GINOTT

371.1
G493t

COLLIER BOOKS
MACMILLAN PUBLISHING COMPANY
NEW YORK

MAXWELL MACMILLAN CANADA
TORONTO

MAXWELL MACMILLAN INTERNATIONAL
NEW YORK   OXFORD   SINGAPORE   SYDNEY

To Aliska

Copyright © 1972 by Congruent Communication, Incorporated

All rights reserved. No part of this book may be reproduced or transmitted in any form or by any means, electronic or mechanical, including photocopying, recording, or by any information storage and retrieval system, without permission in writing from the Publisher.

Collier Books
Macmillan Publishing Company
866 Third Avenue
New York, NY 10022

Maxwell Macmillan Canada, Inc.
1200 Eglinton Avenue East
Suite 200
Don Mills, Ontario M3C 3N1

Macmillan Publishing Company is part of the Maxwell Communication Group of Companies.

Library of Congress Cataloging-in-Publication Data
Ginott, Haim G.
    Teacher and child : a book for parents and teachers / Haim G. Ginott.—
1st Collier Books ed.
        p.   cm.
    Includes bibliographical references and index.
        ISBN 0-02-013974-8
        1. Teacher-student relationships.   2. Home and school.   I. Title.
    LB1033.G5   1993   92-45796   CIP
    371.1'023–dc20

Macmillan books are available at special discounts for bulk purchases for sales promotions, premiums, fund-raising, or educational use. For details, contact:

Special Sales Director
Macmillan Publishing Company
866 Third Avenue
New York, NY 10022

First Collier Books Edition 1993

10   9   8   7   6   5   4

Printed in the United States of America

❋ CONTENTS

N.C. WESLEYAN COLLEGE
ELIZABETH BRASWELL PEARSALL LIBRARY

8 *Contents*

INTRODUCTION

Haim Ginott died on November 4, 1973, after a long and painful illness. He was fifty-one years old. The last book he wrote, *Teacher and Child*, is being reissued on the twentieth anniversary of his death.

A few weeks before he died he looked at his three books—*Between Parent and Child, Between Parent and Teenager*, and *Teacher and Child*—that had revolutionized the way parents and teachers talk to children, and said to me, "Alice, you'll see, my books will be classics." His prediction has come true.

Before he became a psychologist, Haim Ginott was an elementary school teacher in Holon, Israel. He was a graduate of the David Yellin Teachers College in Jerusalem, but after teaching for a few years he realized that he was not sufficiently prepared to deal with "live" children in the classroom. As he would say, "I tried to teach them to be polite and they were rude; to be neat and they were messy; to be cooperative and they were disruptive." It was then that he decided to come to the United States, to Columbia University Teachers College. But their education courses were not helpful, either. He knew that, like most teachers, he came to the profession with the best of intentions; but what he lacked were the skills to fulfill those intentions, to be able to function in the classroom humanely as well as effectively. He wanted to learn how to discipline without humiliating; how to criticize without destroying self-worth; how to praise without judging; how to express anger without hurting; how to acknowledge, not argue with, feelings; how to respond so that children would learn to trust their inner reality and develop self-confidence.

"What is the goal of education?" he would ask. "When all is said and done, we want children to grow up to be decent human beings, a 'mensch,' a person with compassion, commitment, and caring." How then does one go about humanizing a child, making a "mensch" out of him? Only by using "menschy" methods: By recognizing that the process is the method, that the ends do not justify the means, and that in our attempt to get children to behave in a way that is conducive to learning, we do not damage them psychologically. Also, that we do not talk to children in a way that will enrage them, diminish their self-confidence, inflict hurt, or cause them to lose faith in their competence and ability. Because children learn what they experience. They are like wet cement. Any word that falls on them makes an impact. Children are especially vulnerable. What a parent or teacher says even in jest can have serious consequences in their lives.

It was only as a child psychotherapist that Haim Ginott was able to develop the communication skills that enabled him to listen and talk to children in a special manner, to enter into their world in a compassionate and understanding way and then share this knowledge with parents and teachers. As he said, "I'm a child psychotherapist. I treat disturbed children and they improve. What is it that I do that helps? I communicate with them in a unique way. If caring communication can drive sick children sane, its principles and practices belong to teachers and parents. While psychotherapists can cure, only those in daily contact with children can prevent them from needing psychological help. But first they have to become aware and then discard their language of rejection and learn a language of acceptance."

Parents and teachers even know the words. They heard their parents use them with guests and strangers. It was a language that was protective of feelings, not critical of behavior. What does a teacher say to a guest who comes to her classroom and forgets her umbrella? Does he run after her and say, "What is the matter with you? Every time you come to visit you forget something. If it's not one thing it's another. You're forty-four years old! When will you ever learn? I bet you'd forget your head if it were not attached to your neck. Why can't you be like your sister? She knows how to behave responsibly!" That's not what teachers say to a guest. They say, "Here's your umbrella." They give information without derogation.

Teachers and parents need to change priorities. It's those whose welfare has been entrusted to them who deserve the best. And the best is the most civilized. Words that generate love, not hate; diminish dissension, not destroy desire; humor, not enrage.

But many teachers and parents were confused when they listened to Haim Ginott or read his books. They couldn't decide whether he was strict or permissive. They were concerned that if they started to relate to children in a caring way they would have to sacrifice setting limits and setting standards, that the children would become undisciplined.

Haim Ginott was both strict and permissive. He was strict when it came to behavior. There was acceptable and unacceptable behavior. Parents and teachers had to decide for themselves what behavior they would or would not tolerate. But he was permissive when it came to feelings, the positive, negative, and ambivalent. Because neither children nor adults can help how they feel. He used to say, "Birds fly, fish swim, and people feel." That is how we are. It's therefore not in anyone's best interest to make children feel uncomfortable or, even more seriously, guilty for the way they feel.

When a child says to a parent "I hate my teacher!" it's destructive to try to deny or argue with the way he or she feels by saying, "No, you don't! How can you hate her, after all she's done for you! Besides, in this home we don't hate, we only love." Not only will the child not stop hating her teacher, but the adult has missed the opportunity to find out what is bothering the child. It's better for children's mental health when their feelings are acknowledged: "Your teacher has made you very angry. Would you like to tell me what happened?"

Over the years many parents and teachers studied with Haim Ginott in New York and Florida. They contributed to his understanding, providing many of the anecdotes in the book that illustrate his principles of communication. They, on the other hand, benefitted from his wisdom, his warmth, and his humor. They also took home with them and into the classroom some wise sayings that helped them in times of crisis, such as: The beginning of wisdom is silence, and then comes listening. Authority calls for brevity. Learn to talk less and listen more. When things go wrong, it's not a good time to teach lessons ("When someone is drowning it's not a good time to teach them how to swim"). Don't blame, look for solutions. Try to respond to complaints without being defensive or countercomplaining. Avoid embarrassing questions. Talk to the heart, not the mind.

Although English was not Haim Ginott's native tongue, he loved the English language. He loved it as a poet, using it sparingly and with precision. Like the early masters he dispensed his wisdom in parables, allegories, and epigrams: "Don't be a teacher; be a human being who is a teacher."

A story is told about a rabbi who died at the age of forty-eight. When the family returned from the funeral the eldest son said, "Our father had a long life." Everyone was aghast. "How can you say that of a man who died so young?" The son responded, "Because his life was full; he wrote many important books and touched many lives."

That is my consolation.

Alice Ginott, Ph.D.

❋ PREFACE

Teachers are expected to reach unattainable goals with inadequate tools. The miracle is that at times they accomplish this impossible task. Schools, however, cannot survive on miracles. Every teacher deserves effective tools and skills. The question is: Can psychology provide them? Can therapeutic concepts be translated into specific educational practices?

This book says, "Yes." On the basis of techniques developed in child therapy and tested in the classroom, concrete suggestions and practical solutions are offered for dealing with daily situations and psychological problems faced by all teachers.

The philosophy of this book is best summed up in the following words, written by the author as a young teacher: "I have come to a frightening conclusion. I am the decisive element in the classroom. It is my personal approach that creates the climate. It is my daily mood that makes the weather. As a teacher I possess tremendous power to make a child's life miserable or joyous. I can be a tool of torture or an instrument of inspiration. I can humiliate or humor, hurt or heal. In all situations it is

my response that decides whether a crisis will be
escalated or de-escalated, and a child humanized or
de-humanized."

Many teaching problems will be solved in the
next few decades. There will be new learning environments and new means of instruction. One function, however, will always remain with the teacher:
to create the emotional climate for learning. No
machine, sophisticated as it may be, can do this job.

Computer instruction is still in the future. To
benefit from it schools may have to wait for the
twenty-first century. No such wait, however, is necessary for teachers to become experts in effective and
affective education. For a change, human knowledge
can precede technological development.

✳ A NOTE TO READERS

The encounters in this book between teacher and child are depicted in short scenarios. *They are not meant to be taken literally.* They serve only as practical guides to principles of communication. Teachers' responses are to be tailored with ingenuity, according to person and situation. I want to thank the teachers and parents in my seminars who recorded their struggle for new attitudes, concepts, and language and shared them with the readers of this book.

Haiku

Child, give me your hand
That I may walk in the light
Of your faith in me.

HANNAH KAHN

CHAPTER 1

Teachers Talk About Themselves

A Theme of Despair.
Until the System Changes.

A THEME OF DESPAIR

A group of teachers met to discuss life in the classroom. They were young in years and experience but already disillusioned. Some of them thought of dropping out and quitting the profession. Others decided to stay on but quit caring. All of them vented their feelings with authenticity and vigor. They pulled no punches.

ANN: After one year of experience, I've decided: I am not fit for my job. I came to teaching full of love and fantasy. Now, the illusions have evaporated and the love has gone. Teaching is not a profession. It's slow murder, death in daily installments.

BOB: Welcome to the club: "The Postgraduate Dropouts." If I told you how I hate my job, you would think I am crazy. I am a music teacher. I love music. It's my life. But I dream of burning the school and playing the fiddle

at the fire. I detest the principal, I despise my
supervisor, and I hate the system. I want to get
out fast and alive.

CLARA: I am so sad I could cry. I am disappointed
and disenchanted, because I expected so much.
I wanted to do good. I wanted to change the
child, the school, the neighborhood, the world.
How naïve! I smiled at rattlesnakes and they
bit me, and now I too am full of poison.

DORIS: I thought I loved kids, especially the children
of the poor. I was aching to plunge in and give
them my best, make up for their deprivation,
convince them that they are smart and worth-
while. Instead they convinced me that I am
dumb and weak.

EARL: I had no illusions, so I'm not disappointed.
I knew the kids were rotten and the system
corrupt. I never expected my efforts to make
a difference. You are all so heartbroken: you
wanted to empty the ocean with a broken ladle
and you found out: mission impossible.

DORIS: Why did you become a teacher?

EARL: It's a job. If you don't take it to heart, it's not
that bad. I like short hours, long vacations, and
fringe benefits.

CLARA: God save us.

EARL: Don't get sanctimonious with me. I'm not the
one who hates his job. I know the system and
have no false hopes. It's a racket. I don't like it

but I don't fight it. I live with it and get all I can from it.

FLORENCE: Every day I come to school full of energy. I return home half dead. The noise drives me mad. It drowns out everything: my philosophy of education, my theories of learning, and all my good will. It stupefies me and blinds me. And all the time I am aware that I am under surveillance by Big Brother's probing eye and ever-present ear.

GRACE: Every day I say to myself, "This is going to be a peaceful day. I am not going to get involved. I am not going to be provoked, lose my temper, and ruin my health." But every day I lose control of myself in the classroom and return home depressed and disgusted with myself. Like a computer, I follow programmed instructions, I obey coded commands: "Yell your heart out. Get hysterical! Go mad!"

HAROLD: I want to educate children to work for peace. The irony is that I am continuously embroiled in battles with them. It just doesn't make sense to me.

EARL: Are you trying to be rational? To make sense? It's a mad world. School is a perfect preparation for this world. To approach the system rationally is like trying to kill yourself by rules of reason.

DORIS: I work in a poor neighborhood. People are

N.C. WESLEYAN COLLEGE
ELIZABETH BRASWELL PEARSALL LI

prompt to take offense. They suspect you are slighting them. I have learned to listen and nod my head. I'm afraid to talk.

ANN: I tried to be fair to all children, but I soon found that attitudes are stronger than intentions. I could not stand the bullies and the wise guys. I suppose they too needed sympathy and guidance, but I couldn't help them. I felt more like killing them, and they knew it.

EARL: Strange, I like assertive children, but I can't stand the weak and meek and runny-nosed. I get angry at their whining. "Why don't you wipe your nose, stand up and fight?" I want to say.

HAROLD: The gulf between knowledge and practice is almost unbridgeable. An ancient philosopher said, "Authority allied with affection is more powerful than that founded on force." Yet we use force and instill hate. Our principal says, "Let them hate you as long as they obey you." But we all know that children do not learn readily from a teacher they hate.

GRACE: Perhaps I didn't teach the children much, but I've learned a lot about myself. I never knew I was so middle-class. I never suspected I had such strong needs for order, neatness, and quiet. I was confronted with wild kids, much more energetic than I. After a while, I couldn't stand the yelling, the fighting, the profanity. I felt embarrassed and humiliated. And I suffered anxiety and panic. This was my autumn of anguish, my winter of discontent, my spring of despair.

BOB: You are a poet. No wonder the system kills you. It murders anything decent in us. There is no place for sensitive people in public schools.

GRACE: I could not get used to their language and conduct. The wanton destruction, dirty messes, and four-letter words! For some of my children "mother" is only half a word. Most of the year I was on the brink of a breakdown, fighting my anger and panic. I used to pray each morning, "Please, God, don't let me go mad in front of the children." The battle for self-control exhausted my energy. It left me drained, emotionally and physically. I agree with Bob and Earl: teaching belongs to the tough and to those who don't care.

CLARA: I didn't fail teaching. It failed me. Every day I prepared my lessons and was eager to teach. Every day something happened that disrupted my plans. It takes only one clown to infect a class, one smart aleck to ruin a lesson. Hell, I hate these kids.

IRA: Your trouble is that you entered the field of education—

CLARA (*interrupting*): You are damn right.

IRA:—with missionary zeal and a rush to the rescue.

You "adore" little children and want to save their poor souls.

CLARA: What's wrong with that?

IRA: You make a lousy teacher. You are easily hurt. The children activate your own past pains, and you melt in your own misery. The first requirement of a teacher is strength. Then you can be good. If you are weak and good you only engender sadism and invite attacks.

EARL: I agree with you. I have seen teachers oozing love and creating hate.

DORIS: Isn't our love good enough any more?

IRA: Loving is a complicated process. Children accustomed to rejection are frightened by love. They are suspicious of closeness that is forced on them. They need a teacher who is willing to remain at a safe distance.

BOB: Thanks for the mini-course in child psychology. But you do make sense. I too have noticed the failure of overeager, overinvolved teachers. They are enmeshed in stormy relations. They are distressed if a child feels unhappy and overjoyed if he makes progress. Teaching is their personal pursuit of happiness. They use pupils to gratify private needs. They often go from too-intense positive to too-intense negative feelings. The child gets confused.

DORIS: I notice that we have moved from discussing our feelings to talking about other teachers. What about our attitudes toward teaching now that we have had some experience?

ANN: I look back in anger at the last year—the wasted time, the listless hours, the long conferences, the futile talks. Our principal loves vagueness and adores ambiguity. He delays decisions and postpones life. Whenever he is pressed for action, he retreats into more words, which become more and more abstract. Talking to him gives me the sensation of drowning in a sea of words.

HAROLD: I visited a prison last week, and I came back bothered and burdened. I can't escape thinking about my responsibility as a teacher. Every adult murderer was once a child who spent years in school. Every thief had teachers who presumably taught him values and morals. Every criminal was educated by teachers. Every prison is a dramatic demonstration of the failure of our system. We need to take a good look at the landscape of our responsibility.

DORIS: I remember how teachers taught us dishonesty. They never accepted a simple truth. They insisted on a lie that was both believable and interesting.

HAROLD: Education is a lost cause. There are solutions but they'll never be used. Effective remedies require a fundamental change in the system. The bosses will never allow it.

EARL: The whole system of education is built on distrust. The teacher distrusts the students. The principal distrusts the teachers. The superintendent suspects the principals, and the school board is wary of the superintendent. Each authority sets up rules and regulations that create a prison atmosphere and an implicit charge that everyone in the system is dishonest or incompetent or irresponsible.

DORIS: That's how students become con men. They learn to figure out what the teacher wants and give it to him. The teachers dope out what the principal wants. For instance, my principal is not interested in how I teach or what kind of person I am. If the records of attendance and grades are in order and on time, he is satisfied.

IRA: Your stories sound so depressing. I wonder why millions of teachers keep on teaching year after year. They can't all be confirmed masochists. Are there no satisfactions in our job?

DORIS: You tell me, if you can.

IRA: I certainly can, but I'm not sure if it'll convince you.

DORIS: Go ahead, try me.

IRA: O.K. I have difficulties just like you. But I also

enjoy feeling needed, getting to know what
makes children tick, and learning to understand myself better.

EARL: You have it down pat, don't you?

IRA: Sorry it sounds pat to you. To me, it rings more
like an agonizing appraisal.

EARL: Any more words of wisdom?

IRA: Plenty! But I'll share with you only one truth:
There is no place for cynics in elementary
school. The young need protection from adults
with stone souls.

EARL: Bravo. Bravissimo. That's the spirit, Dr.
Spock.

BOB: I freeze every time the principal enters my
class. This cold fish tells me to be more warm
with children. I'm too somber, he says. I need
to be more alive. With him around I feel dead.
He has sympathy for the poor children, he
says. Well, I am poor. Why doesn't he show
some sympathy for me? Why doesn't he demonstrate warmth? Right now, I myself could use
some warm words.

HAROLD: My supervisor loves books and papers and
research. Only people he hates. He knows all
about education in ancient Athens and in
medieval Rome. But how to supervise a live
teacher—that he doesn't know.

ANN: Our faculty is full of people killing time, wait-

ing for retirement. They are old at middle age.
They are bitter, going nowhere and crying over
their spilled lives.

DORIS: One old teacher keeps giving me advice:
escape while you are young. Look at me and
run for your life. Teaching will kill you. It'll
murder your spirit, drain your energy, and cor-
rode your character. The daily battles with
children, the constant complaining by parents,
the ceaseless carping of the A.P.—what do you
need them for? Choose yourself a respectable
career.

HAROLD: I became aware that college failed to prepare me for my job. Teaching children takes
at least as much skill as flying a jet. In college
they taught us to drive a tractor, while telling
us it was a jet. No wonder we crash every time
we try to take off.

DORIS: How true. My professors talked about children's needs, parents' needs, and society's
needs. I wish they had made me aware of my
needs. They made me believe that children
come to school with a terrific thirst for knowledge. All I had to do was to quench their thirst.
Now I know better. Children come to school to
make my life miserable, and they succeed.

BOB: We all feel deeply disappointed, because our
initial experience is not what we had expected.
Teaching is like taking a plane to a tropical

island and landing in the Arctic. It's quite a shock to expect sunshine and to face a long, cold, polar winter.

CLARA: Is there no hope at all for education?

EARL: There ain't. Get it through your head, girl, and you'll live longer.

IRA: If there is no hope for education, there is no hope for humanity. I can't accept such nihilism. I have faith in our ingenuity and inventiveness. Solutions will be found in education itself—in better education, in different education.

UNTIL THE SYSTEM CHANGES

The preceding discussion is highly uniform; the stress does not change, and the mood is monotonous. The monotony only emphasizes the main motif: the dissatisfaction, disappointment, and despair of young teachers. Their pain comes from the nature of life in school. They weep, to quote Virgil, "because of the tears of things."

Some of the teachers lose faith and give up hope. Others clamor for reform. The more radical seek to change systems in midstream. The more conservative pursue palliatives. Meanwhile life in the classroom marches on: There are children to teach, parents to appease, and principals to account to. They all make demands on teachers' time and energy. How to survive with dignity is not a rhetorical question for a teacher

There is a story about a man in dire trouble who came to his rabbi for help. The rabbi listened and advised, "Trust in God. He will provide for you." "Yes," answered the man. "But tell me, what do I do until then?"

Teachers ask similar questions: "How can I survive until the system changes?" "What can I do today to improve life in the classroom?"

This book attempts to answer these questions.

At Their Best

Theory and Practice. A Note of Comfort.
"Everything Is Going Wrong."
Help with Algebra. "I'm Always Gypped."
Minimal Intervention. A Reassuring Tune.
Respect for Art. Stage Fright.
"Mahatma Gandhi." A Helpful Dialogue.
Consolation without Explanation. First Aid.
A Gentle Note. A Minor Tantrum.
Benign Correction. Focusing on Feelings.
Conferring Dignity. A Modest Aim.

THEORY AND PRACTICE

A story is told about a philosopher who was crossing a big river on a small boat. He asked the boatman, "Do you know philosophy?" "I can't say I do," answered the man. "You lost one third of your life," said the philosopher. "Do you know any literature?" he persisted. "I can't say I do," answered the man. "You lost two thirds of your life," proclaimed the philosopher. At that moment the boat hit a rock and started sinking. "Do you know how to swim?" asked the boatman. "No," replied the philosopher. "Then you lost your whole life," said the man.

When crucial problems appear, philosophies often disappear. To a man in a sinking boat, theory is irrelevant. Either he knows how to swim or he drowns. In the midst of classroom crises, all the books in all the libraries are of no help. All the lectures and all the courses are of little value. At the moment of truth, only skill saves.

What counts in education is attitudes expressed
in skills. The attitudes that count are known. In
fact, teachers are tired of hearing about them again
and again at every conference and convention. As
one teacher put it: "I already know what a child
needs. I know it by heart. He needs to be accepted,
respected, liked, and trusted; encouraged, supported, activated, and amused; able to explore,
experiment, and achieve. Damn it! He needs too
much. All I lack is Solomon's wisdom, Freud's insight, Einstein's knowledge, and Florence Night-
ingale's dedication."

In theory, we already know what good education is. We have all the concepts. Unfortunately,
one cannot educate children on conceptions alone.
Children present problems which do not disappear,
even when the teacher believes in democracy, love,
respect, acceptance, individual differences, and personal uniqueness. Though magnificent, these concepts are too abstract and too large. They are like
a thousand-dollar bill—good currency, but useless in
meeting mundane needs such as buying a cup of
coffee, taking a cab, or making a phone call. For
daily life, one needs coins. For classroom commerce,
teachers needs psychological small change. They
need specific skills for dealing effectively and
humanely with minute-to-minute happenings—the
small irritations, the daily conflicts, the sudden
crises. All these situations call for helpful and realis-
tic reactions. A teacher's response has crucial con-

sequences. It creates a climate of compliance or defiance, a mood of contentment or contention, a desire to make amends or to take revenge. It affects the child's conduct and character for better or for worse.

These are the facts of emotional life which make teaching and learning possible or impossible. At their best, teachers recognize this core truth: Learning is always in the present tense, and it is always personal. The following vignettes illustrate teachers at their best.

A NOTE OF COMFORT

A teacher distributed new books to her class. The supply ran out before Paul Z., age nine, got his book. He melted into tears. "I am always the last one to get anything," he protested. "Because my name starts with a Z, I get zero. I hate my name. I hate school. I hate everybody." Paul's teacher wondered how to be of immediate help. She wrote him a note:

> Dear Paul,
>   I know how sad you must feel. You waited for your new book eagerly, and suddenly—such a disappointment. Everyone got a book except you. I personally am

going to see to it that you receive your new
book.

> Sincerely,
> Your Teacher

Paul calmed down, comforted by his teacher's
warm words. He will long remember this kind
moment.

Had the teacher had a different orientation,
such as: "Children ought to learn early how to take
disappointments in stride," she would probably
have escalated his hurt. "Why do you make such a
big deal over a book? You didn't get it today. So
you'll get it tomorrow. You are nine years old and
still such a crybaby."

This approach would have increased Paul's
bitterness against his unkind teacher and unfair
fate.

"EVERYTHING IS GOING WRONG"

It was Wendy's first day in fifth grade. The
teacher showed her where to get her English books.
When Wendy touched the bookcase, all the books
came tumbling down. Wendy started to cry.

TEACHER: Wendy, the books have fallen down. We
need to pick them up.

WENDY: I spoiled my first day in school. Everything is going wrong.

TEACHER: It has been a rough morning for you.

WENDY: It sure has. Do you want to hear what's happened?

TEACHER: Tell me.

The teacher helped Wendy pick up the books, while Wendy talked about her difficult morning. The first day ended on a pleasant note.

In this incident the teacher was most helpful. She did not criticize. She pointed out what needed to be done. She talked succinctly and listened sympathetically.

HELP WITH ALGEBRA

Ada, age fourteen, found it difficult to understand algebra. She felt ashamed, too shy to ask for help. The teacher noticed her reticence and offered assistance discreetly and graciously:

He said: "Ada, algebra is a very difficult subject. You have to use symbolic solutions. You have to substitute numbers for figures and to remember to change signs when a number is moved from one side of the equation to the other. You may need help with algebra. Ask me when the occasion demands."

Ada's teacher was both kind and competent. He

asked no questions, made no accusations, and gave no empty assurances. Instead he conveyed empathy and described processes.

"I'M ALWAYS GYPPED"

Gym period was over. The teacher told the group to stop their basketball game. Joseph protested, "Everyone had more chances than I. I'm always gypped." The teacher said, "To change your feelings about this situation, take three more shots. I'll wait for you."

Joseph did not believe his own ears. He quickly curved the ball into the basket and then brought it back to his teacher. He seemed pleased and contented.

The beneficial ingredient in this incident was the teacher's attitude. He was flexible and sympathetic. The child's feelings were more important to him than rigid rules.

MINIMAL INTERVENTION

June was dissatisfied with the topic assigned to her in Social Studies. When she requested a new topic, the teacher said, "June, I see this topic is not to your liking. You aren't that interested in Egyptian religion. You love art. Gina was assigned Egyptian art. Talk it over with her and see if you can exchange or cooperate on your assignments."

June thanked the teacher for understanding her desire and proceeded to negotiate with Gina.

A REASSURING TUNE

Nine-year-old Anne was one of thirty children at a piano recital at her teacher's home. She felt forlorn and looked teary. She withdrew into a corner and refused conversation and refreshments. The teacher noticed Anne's distress.

TEACHER: Anne, blue is a very becoming color for you.

ANNE: I didn't think you noticed my dress. How can you notice everybody? I never imagined—you have so many children.

TEACHER: You are all my students, and I notice every one of you.

ANNE (*on the verge of tears*): It doesn't seem possible. I bet you have favorites—like the kids who play the best. I'm only a beginner.

TEACHER: My love is not measured by your height,

or weight, or grade. I have enough love for all
my students.

ANNE (*smiling a little*): I bet no one makes you the
drawings I do—and they're all original.

TEACHER: I can tell they are original, and I enjoy
looking at them.

Anne's sad expression disappeared. Later, she
played beautifully. When she left she was beaming,
busy chatting with the other children.

RESPECT FOR ART

The teacher saw a caricature of his face on the
blackboard. It was sharp, accurate, and funny. The
class waited for his reaction.

He observed it with interest and then said: "It
is too well done to be erased. Let the artist first
copy it on paper. My compliments to the talented
caricaturist."

This teacher demonstrated maturity. He took
no personal offense at the biting picture. He was
not hurt by a child's prank. He did not look for the
culprit, nor did he try to shame him. He avoided
fruitless preaching and moralizing. Instead he
encouraged creativity and showed respect for art.

STAGE FRIGHT

The class was rehearsing the play *Peter Pan*. Ralph, playing Captain Hook, developed stage fright. He told his teacher that he was no longer interested in the part. The teacher said, "It seems to me that you are not happy about certain words you have to say in this play. Change them to suit you." Ralph omitted one self-disparaging phrase and the words "my beauty" when addressing a girl. He kept his part in the play.

The teacher's skill saved the situation. She did not argue with Ralph or try to change his mind. She evoked no guilt ("How can you let us down? We counted on you."). Instead she showed sensitivity and remained solution-oriented.

"MAHATMA GANDHI"

A substitute teacher asked a boy for his name. He replied, "Mahatma Gandhi." The class burst out in loud laughter. The teacher said: "Mahatma Gandhi is a good person to want to emulate and be like." The class calmed down. The teacher went on with her task.

The teacher's competence . saved time and

effort. In the hands of a punitive teacher this incident could have turned into a bitter exchange and discipline problem.

A HELPFUL DIALOGUE

NINA (*age five*): Teacher, you had a baby, right?

TEACHER: You remember it.

NINA: You're married. You're a "Mrs." and you wear a ring.

TEACHER: You observed that.

NINA: My sister's going to have a baby.

TEACHER: You're going to be an aunt.

NINA: Yes, but my sister's not married.

TEACHER: Oh.

NINA: Is it better to be married when you have a baby?

TEACHER: You're wondering about that?

NINA: Yes. Everybody at home was all upset and mad, but I'm happy.

TEACHER: You're looking forward to being an aunt.

NINA: Yes, but I wish everyone was happy.

TEACHER: You wish they shared your joy.

NINA: Yeah.

Nina paused for a moment, ran over to her teacher, and hugged her.

In this dialogue the teacher was most helpful. She understood Nina's messages and mirrored her feelings. She gave her credit for her observations and reflected her hidden wishes. Nina felt so understood, accepted, and appreciated that she reciprocated with a gesture of love.

CONSOLATION WITHOUT EXPLANATION

This incident was related by a third-grade teacher:

"On lunch duty, whenever a child approached me crying, I consoled him instead of prying into etiology. The tears would cease. A changed look would appear on the child's face, as if saying: 'You understand. Thank you!'

"I was in the lunchroom when Ramon, age eight, came in crying uncontrollably. It was difficult to discern the reason for his grief. But then I realized that it really didn't matter. He had come for *comfort*, not for *diagnosis*. I stroked the back of his head and said, "I know, Ramon, I know." Slowly he regained his composure as I uttered various sympathies. He did not find it necessary to explain why he was crying, but managed a small smile and went back to his seat."

FIRST AID

Stephen, age seven, worked hard on a clay boat. He molded it, made oars, and put people in it. He wanted to show his proud possession to the teacher. As he approached the teacher, Bruce bumped into him. The boat fell and broke into many pieces. Stephen burst into tears. He attacked Bruce in a blinding rage. The teacher knew how to administer emotional first aid. He separated the boys and focused on Stephen's hurt. He said, "I saw you working on your boat. I know how much effort you put in it. It hurts to see it destroyed. Here is some new clay to make another boat when you are in the mood."

The teacher intentionally ignored Stephen's outburst. He also abstained from blaming Bruce, or questioning his motives. He concentrated on comforting Stephen, thus helping him regain self-control and self-esteem.

A GENTLE NOTE

A note arrived from the school nurse summoning Lea, age eight, for a vaccination. Lea started crying.

TEACHER: It's scary to get a vaccination.

LEA: Yes.

TEACHER: You wish you didn't have to go to the nurse.

LEA: Yes. I am scared.

TEACHER: I know. Let me write a note to the nurse and ask her to be especially gentle with you.

The teacher wrote the note and Lea went to the nurse. When Lea came back, tearful and red-eyed, the teacher said, "It hurt, didn't it?" "Yes," said Lea. "It hurt bad at first, but it's better now."

This teacher was most helpful. She did not make light of Lea's fears ("A big girl like you afraid of a little vaccine?"). She did not use cold logic ("You need it for your own good."). She did not offer false assurance ("It won't hurt at all. It's only a scratch."). Instead, she recognized feelings, acknowledged wishes, and offered a helpful gesture.

A MINOR TANTRUM

Russell, age seven, was disgruntled because he had not been called on during a word game in class. When the game was over, he threw a minor tantrum.

RUSSELL: You like the other children better than me.

TEACHER: You really feel that way, don't you, Russell?

RUSSELL: Yes. You never call on me.

TEACHER: You want me to call on you more often. You want to have a chance more often.

RUSSELL: Yes.

TEACHER: Thank you, Russell, for bringing your feelings to my attention. I'll make a note of the way you feel so I won't forget.

In this incident, the teacher demonstrated competence. She did not deny the child's feeling. She did not counterattack. She did not admonish or punish. Instead, she won over the child.

BENIGN CORRECTION

David, age nine, showed his homework to his teacher.

TEACHER (*noticing a mistake*): These problems need to be checked again.

DAVID: You are looking at me as if I am stupid.

TEACHER: Let me change my look to a more benign one.

DAVID: What's benign?

TEACHER: Gentle and gracious. Your assignment

was so difficult. There were many problems. It took time and effort to do what you have done.

DAVID: Yeah, it sure did.

David checked the problems and corrected the errors. A good mood prevailed.

The teacher's benign response averted argument and acrimony. When attacked, she became neither offensive nor defensive. She did not counterattack nor did she deny David's accusations. She chose to switch rather than fight. She altered the context of the conversation by giving appreciation instead of an explanation.

FOCUSING ON FEELINGS

Rudy, age seven, started crying suddenly. The teacher went over to him and said, "Something is the matter."

He nodded and pointed to his new toy car. "The wheels were knocked off. Julio did it," he cried.

"By accident," Julio chimed.

"It's your new car, Rudy, isn't it?" the teacher said with concern.

"Yes," replied Rudy.

"Oh my," said the teacher.

Rudy stopped crying. He was silent for a few

minutes, then he said, "Well, I have another car at home."

The crisis was over.

This incident demonstrates the power of succinct and specific sympathy. The teacher avoided questions, accusations, and lessons. She did not ask Rudy why he brought the car to school, or Julio why he broke it. Instead she focused on feelings. Reality took care of itself.

CONFERRING DIGNITY

Susan, age twelve, volunteered to assist in cataloguing the books in the school library during the weekend. On Saturday she realized that she was swamped with homework. She regretted her promise, and felt disgruntled and depressed. When she arrived at the library that morning, she was full of tears. Her teacher listened to her story with attentive silence. Then she said, "Feeling so disheartened, you still came to work. That's discipline. That's character. That's integrity." The teacher's words brought instant balm to Susan. She felt like a heroine, a remarkable person, a responsible individual.

This episode could have had a less fortunate ending had the teacher responded with moralizing or minimizing comments:

"Why did you leave a week's homework for the last minute?"

"Why did you volunteer if you knew you had so much work?"

"Next time think twice before you volunteer."

"You probably would have wasted your time today, anyway."

"In the library, maybe you'll learn something."

It was the teacher's ability to convey respect and to confer dignity that saved the situation. Her short response communicated to Susan that her work was valued and her character cherished.

A MODEST AIM

Teachers at their best display a common orientation: They do not believe in the power of pontification. They neither preach nor moralize. They give no guilt and demand no promises. They do not dig into etiologies of minor misbehavior or pry into causes of classroom incidents. They are not preoccupied with the child's past history or distant future. They deal with the present. What matters to them is the here and now of a child in distress. As one teacher put it, "I used to focus on future developments. Now I have a more modest aim: I am concerned with present moods and prevailing needs. Instead of distant utopias, I want to achieve minute-to-minute humanness in my classroom."

Teachers at their best are a living proof that such a transformation is possible and practical.

CHAPTER 3

At Their Worst

"Are You Naturally Slow?"

Esthetics with a Sledgehammer.

Long Division. Name-Calling.

Invasion of Privacy. A Biting Inquiry.

Not a Laughing Matter.

What's in a Name? A Poisoned Pen.

"Don't You Know Anything?"

"Listen, Van Gogh."

"A Teacher Shouldn't Talk Like That."

War About Peace.

A Lost Lesson in Fair Play. A Torn Coat.

A Private Pogrom. A Mother's Testimony.

Is There Hope?

A famous photographer told a friend about the anguish and despair of a poor Indian hamlet. "The women were pregnant, the children sick, and the men out of work. The village was a ruin and the land a wreck." "What did *you* do?" asked the friend. "I shot them in color," answered the photographer.

Unlike this cameraman, a teacher cannot hide behind a role. Though a professional, he is a concerned human being first and always. As a teacher he acts appropriately in stressful situations. He shows "grace under pressure"; he responds insightfully. He does not react impulsively.

All teachers work hard; children make demands and teachers have to respond endlessly. Some teachers, however, work too hard. They spend time and waste energy on battles that can be avoided, on skirmishes that can be skirted, and on wars that can be prevented. In each school there is a gigantic waste of human resources. Time and talent are devoured by needless conflicts and useless quarrels.

The following vignettes demonstrate the destructive power of inappropriate comments and acts in everyday classroom situations.

"ARE YOU NATURALLY SLOW?"

"Take your seats," said the teacher to his class. But one boy remained standing in the aisle. Angrily the teacher turned on him: "Alfred! What are you waiting for—a special invitation? Why must you *always* be the last one? Why does it take you forever to sit down? Are you naturally slow or is someone helping you?" Alfred winced and sat down.

The teacher began reading a poem, but Alfred did not hear it. He was preoccupied with more prosaic images. He visualized his teacher dead and was totally absorbed with the funeral arrangements.

There is no place for cutting comments between teacher and child. They only evoke hate and revenge fantasies. The teacher could have made a simple, declarative statement of his intentions: "Alfred, I am about to read a poem." Most children respond positively to such hints. If Alfred persisted, the teacher could have expressed his annoyance and expectation, firmly but without attack. "Alfred, when the class is ready to begin, I find it annoying to see you still standing."

ESTHETICS WITH A SLEDGEHAMMER

An art teacher showed two drawings to his students. He asked them to tell which one they liked best. Henry, age twelve, took his time to answer. The teacher said: "We don't have all day. Make up your mind, if you have any." Henry blushed while his classmates giggled.

Playing for laughs at a student's expense is unpedagogic, to say the least. A slow student is not cured by sarcasm. Mental processes are not mended by mockery. Ridicule breeds hate and invites vengeance. In difficult moments, a teacher's prime role is to be helpful. Thus he could have said to hesitant Henry: "It's not easy to decide. It's a hard choice to make. There are elements in both drawings that you like. Which picture appeals more to your heart?"

Art cannot be communicated with a sledge-hammer. Esthetics cannot be taught unesthetically.

LONG DIVISION

Matt, age nine, lost his way in the middle of long division. He asked his teacher for assistance. The teacher answered: "Where were you when I explained this problem? You never listen. You always play. Now you want special attention. You are not the only one here. I can't hold special classes for you." Matt went back to his seat, but he found ways to disturb the class during the rest of the hour.

Though busy, the teacher could have been helpful to Matt. He could have said, "Long division is not easy to grasp. I wish I had the time to explain it to you right now. Let's schedule a time convenient to both of us."

Children often misbehave when they have difficulties with an assignment. They are afraid to ask for assistance. Their experience has taught them that to request help is to risk rebuke. They would rather be punished for acting up than ridiculed for ignorance. A teacher's best antidote to misbehavior is a willingness to be helpful.

NAME-CALLING

Mona, age nine, did not finish her work assignment on time. Her teacher said, "You are lazy, careless, and irresponsible."

After class, Mona said to the teacher, "You evidently don't know me well. I'm not lazy and careless. I care very much about my schoolwork. I try very hard to do my best. I come to your class for only forty minutes; so perhaps you don't know me as my other teachers do."

The teacher responded: "You are a fresh young lady, that's what you are. And you have a big mouth. Tell your mother I want to see her in school, to discuss her loud-mouthed daughter." Mona returned home in tears.

Name-calling is taboo for a pedagogue. It only teaches the child name-calling. It creates feelings of resentment. A child often sees himself through his teacher's eyes. What the teacher says about him has serious consequences.

The teacher would have done well to support Mona's positive self-image. She could have said: "Thank you for telling me that you care about schoolwork. I may have been too hasty in my judgment of you." Such a statement would have restored peace and engendered good will.

INVASION OF PRIVACY

Janet, age eleven, usually vivacious and noisy, sat quiet and brooding at her desk.

TEACHER: What's the matter with you today?
JANET: Nothing.

TEACHER: Come on, you can tell me. I can see something is on your mind. What's bothering you?

JANET: Nothing is bothering me.

TEACHER: Listen. You are like an open book to me. I know your personality. I can tell your moods. You got up on the wrong side of the bed, didn't you?

JANET: *Please.* Stop it.

TEACHER: What kind of talk is that, young lady? I have a mind to teach you a lesson in manners, but I am going to spare you. You are upset, and you don't even know it. I understand you better than you understand yourself.

Janet covered her face and did not utter a word during the rest of the hour.

Janet's teacher may have had good intentions, but he was not helpful. It is always dangerous to play emotional detective. Good taste prohibits prying. Courtesy commands distance. Privacy is not to be intruded upon without invitation or permission. Self-disclosure requires a personal choice and the right to reticence. To tell a child, "I understand you better than you do" is an act of emotional arrogance akin to illegal trespassing. Aid is best given discreetly and succinctly (Can I be of help?). Loud, long, and loquacious offerings are embarrassing. They invite resistance and resentment.

A BITING INQUIRY

Felix, age nine, complained to his teacher that a boy from the sixth grade had hit him over the head with a book.

TEACHER: He just came over and hit you! Just like that! You didn't do anything. You were just an innocent bystander, and he was a perfect stranger.

FELIX (*in tears*): Yes.

TEACHER: I don't believe you. You must have done something. I know you. When it comes to provoking, you are an expert.

FELIX: I didn't do anything. I just stood in the hall, minding my own business.

TEACHER: I'm in the hall every day. No one ever attacks me. How come you always attract trouble? You'd better watch out or one of these days you'll be in very hot water.

Felix put his head on the desk and cried, while his teacher turned to the business of the day.

In this incident the teacher talked when he should have listened. He denied facts when he should have acknowledged experience. He asked questions when he should have mirrored feelings: "It must have hurt awfully."

"It must have made you angry."

"You must have felt furious."

"Write up the whole incident for me, if you want to, and I'll see what I can do about it."

It is always helpful for a child in distress to know that his teacher really understands what he has experienced and endured.

NOT A LAUGHING MATTER

Andy, age ten, was at the blackboard, trying, unsuccessfully, to explain a problem in multiplication. The teacher said: "Whenever you open your mouth you subtract from the sum of human knowledge." The class roared. Andy stood in stony silence. The teacher asked another boy to solve the problem and told Andy to listen with both ears.

Chances are that Andy did not listen even with one ear. His mind was far away from the classroom. Andy had learned to escape adults' attacks by blocking out their words. He learned to live in fantasy, safe from assault.

Instead of luring him out of his isolation, the teacher pushed Andy into further encapsulation. Andy needed instruction in multiplication, not destruction of esteem. Though it is not easy, one must resist the impulse to be clever at another person's expense.

WHAT'S IN A NAME?

A boy named Witt gave the wrong answer to a simple question. The teacher said: "With a little more brains you'd be a half-Witt." The class burst out in thunderous laughter. The boy blushed and went meekly to his seat.

From this session on, the children teased Witt mercilessly. They followed the teacher's lead and improvised on it. They called him "Half-bright," "Half-idiot," etc. They made his life unbearable, until he finally changed schools.

A teacher, like a surgeon, must never slash haphazardly. The damage may be permanent.

A POISONED PEN

Tom, age sixteen, failed an exam in English literature. His teacher, a minor writer, saw an opportunity to practice his craft. He wrote on Tom's exam: "Everything changes; only ignorance lasts. You are a perfect example."

Tom felt devastated. The teacher confirmed to him his feeling of inferiority. He accepted the evaluation without resistance; it fitted his self-image. But he kept on brooding about his destiny and destination. He became depressed, gave up social activities, and finally dropped out of school.

Sarcasm is not good for children. It destroys their self-confidence and self-esteem. Like strychnine, it can be fatal. Bitter irony and biting sarcasm only reinforce the traits they attack.

"DON'T YOU KNOW ANYTHING?"

Carl, age eleven, could not open the window at school. The teacher said, "Can't you even open a window? Don't you know anything?" Carl blushed and went back to his seat, cursing under his breath.

The teacher's response was most damaging. Children are never sure about their abilities. A public attack on intelligence hits their most vulnerable spot. Virulent criticism doesn't motivate children to improve; on the contrary, it ruins their initiative. Carl's teacher could have been more helpful had he addressed himself to the situation.

"Is that window causing trouble again?" he could have asked. Carl would have been relieved, reassured, and spurred to try harder. He would have also liked the teacher for saving him embarrassment.

"LISTEN, VAN GOGH"

TEACHER: Why didn't you do the homework?

RON (*age sixteen*): I have been painting. I was on a creative binge. I didn't want to stop in the middle.

TEACHER: You are a creative genius, aren't you? You couldn't stop painting even for an hour. Listen, Van Gogh! You have creative excuses, that's all. But they won't help you in this class. You may be able to bamboozle your mother, but not me. I am smarter than you, kiddo. I know your kind: barefoot bums with great illusions and no talent.

This attack was unnecessary. It only deepened the gap between teacher and child. Verbal spankings do not improve performance or personality. They only ignite hate.

The teacher would have achieved better results had he shown interest in his student's artistic claim. He might even have learned something about modern art. A respectful exchange of ideas about life and art has more motivation for schoolwork and homework than the most imaginative tongue-lashing.

"A TEACHER SHOULDN'T TALK LIKE THAT"

Steven, age twelve, stabbed Barbara with a pencil. Barbara looked back in anger but said nothing. Steven got the message. This would have been the end of the incident were it not for the teacher. In a loud voice he threatened:

"Once more, Steven, and out you go, for good! I am tired of your constant disruptions. You are a pest."

Embarrassed, Steven dropped his eyes but not before smirking a signal to several close friends, who quickly came to his aid.

"A teacher shouldn't talk like that," exclaimed Rusty. "It's not good for our psyche."

"Don't be a smart aleck," shouted the teacher. "It's none of your business."

"No man is an island unto himself," answered Rusty. "Insults give us an inferiority complex."

"Shut up," yelled the teacher in rage. "You are not your brother's keeper. Just close your trap."

The noise subsided; a heavy silence descended. But the atmosphere was filled with poison.

"Today we are going to discuss concepts of mercy and compassion in the teachings of the old prophets," announced the teacher.

A hollow laughter rose and died quickly in the

class as the teacher began to lecture on the quality of mercy.

This teacher engaged in a series of harmful activities. He intervened unnecessarily. He used threats. He lost his temper. He became rude. He conveyed false values and he demonstrated hypocrisy. His lecture on the virtue of pity was sheer sham: Mercy can only be taught mercifully.

WAR ABOUT PEACE

In a Social Studies class Raul, age fifteen, said, "I think we should quit the United Nations. It accomplishes nothing. It is full of bull. All it does is talk, talk, talk."

The teacher tore into Raul: "You are talking nonsense. You are too young to understand such important matters. What do you know about the UN? Have you read any books on the subject? Or any articles? When did you last read a newspaper? You are an ignoramus. Don't you know that without the UN there is no hope for peace?"

This teacher may be a strong supporter of the UN and its peace mission, but in his reply to Raul he started a new war. His attack incited hate, ignited fury, and invited counterattack. Even under provocation a teacher does not belittle children. He responds with dignity to the feeling and content of their message. "I see you have strong feelings about the UN. You are deeply disillusioned with its performance and disheartened by its failure to act. Still, what's our alternative?"

A LOST LESSON IN FAIR PLAY

Mr. Abel, the gym teacher, and a group of children were playing ball. Suddenly Ted, age eight, started crying. "Why are you crying?" asked the teacher. " 'Cause you never throw the ball to me," whispered Ted. The teacher looked at him with annoyance and said: "You are not the only one in the group. Everyone gets a fair chance. Learn to wait your turn. Don't be such a crybaby." And the teacher threw the ball to another child.

The teacher's verbal lesson in fair play was lost on Ted. A child in tears cannot absorb lectures on democracy. When a child feels aggrieved, it is best to acknowledge his complaint and voice his wish. Thus, Mr. Abel could have said to teary Ted: "Oh, so that's why you are crying. You want me to throw the ball to you now. Here is one coming your way, Ted."

A teacher can risk a kind gesture. There is always a chance it may snowball.

A TORN COAT

While playing, José, age nine, accidentally tore his coat. He ran to the teacher crying hysterically. "My mother will kill me. She'll skin me alive." "Why weren't you more careful?" asked the teacher. "Your mother won't kill you but certainly you deserve punishment." José went to pieces. He threw himself on the floor and cried his heart out. The teacher took this occasion to lecture the class on the need for caution, pointing to José as a negative example.

Above all, a teacher needs to demonstrate humanity. Where others condemn, he consoles. Where others blame, he helps A compassionate teacher would say:

"You are afraid your mother will punish you when she sees the coat. Let me write a note telling her it was an accident." The note might not save José from a beating at home but it would spare him from injury at school.

A PRIVATE POGROM

The following report was written by a student teacher:

"What I witnessed in school today was a private pogrom: one teacher playing havoc with the lives of thirty children. With words as weapons, she caused carnage in the classroom. Mrs. L. started the day with a symbolic whipping of a boy who came late. She moved to castigate a girl who forgot her homework. She then hurled epithets at a child caught copying, before defaming the boy who contributed to this crime. The school day had barely begun but the atmosphere was already poisoned."

A MOTHER'S TESTIMONY

The following report was written by a concerned mother after a one-day visit to her son's class:

"It was Open School Week—a chance to sit in on my son's classes and get the feel of what a school day was like for a seventh-grade boy.

"I arrived at the math class in time to watch the children walk in quietly, find their seats, and open their notebooks. A few of the youngsters chatted softly with each other. Suddenly a young woman in a minidress appeared in the doorway, her brows knit with anger. Without a word, she snapped her fingers and jerked her head in the direction of the hall. The children reassembled their books, shuffled outside the room and lined up. The young woman hissed at them. 'How many times do I have to remind you of the rule? No one may enter this room without a teacher!'

"Meekly, the children filed in again. As they took their seats, she rapped out a rapid-fire commentary: 'I want no trouble from you today, Paul. Jimmy, can you keep your mouth shut for five minutes? I doubt it. Roger, do you have your homework today? Why not? Well, that excuse isn't good enough! All right, now we'll check the homework. Who has the answer to the first problem?' Hands shot up.

" 'Seventy-three?'

" '*No.*'

"Another hand waved wildly. 'Seventy-eight?'

" 'No. Who has it? Let's go.'

" 'Seventy-five?'

" 'Right. There's no reason why so many of you are having trouble with that. We went over it before. Next problem.'

"Again the process was repeated until all the homework was 'checked.' During the remainder of the period, she drilled a smaller group of students on decimal points while the rest of the students worked in their seats.

"When the bell rang, I followed the children to their linguistics class. There the teacher began the lesson by instructing everyone to open his grammar book. In a droning monotone, she explained about adverbial clauses and then directed the class to fill in the workbooks. A few youngsters buzzed among themselves, unsure of the directions. She told them that if they had been paying attention, they'd know what to do.

"When the bell rang again, the children quickly collected their belongings and trudged down the hall to their science class. Soundlessly, they took their seats, opened their notebooks, and waited. Finally the teacher entered, a good-looking young man—impeccably tailored. He frowned, carefully removed his jacket and hung it on the back of a chair. He then picked up a ruler and struck the desk with it. 'Friends,' he announced, 'and those who are not my friends, like Sloan, Katz, and Colombo. What phylum do the following animals belong to?'

"A girl raised her hand. 'Mr. B. . . .'

" 'You're rude!'

" 'But, Mr. B., I raised my hand!'

" 'Yes, and you also opened your big, loud mouth!'

"A rapid-fire drill followed, with the children stumbling over the long Latin names of the various phyla. Each name was accompanied by another whack of the long ruler. Then Mr. B. went to the blackboard and swiftly drew another kind of sea creature and wrote its name and phylum. He warned the class to copy it carefully, as they would be held responsible for recognizing it on the next test.

"Everyone dutifully wrote in his notebook, except one boy who gazed raptly upon the drawing on the blackboard. The boy raised his hand. 'Mr. B.,' he said. 'He has a hole in his shell.'

"Mr. B. looked annoyed. 'Yes, Jeffrey, what of it?'

" 'What's it for?'

" 'I don't know,' Mr. B. snapped. 'It's just there.'

"Jeffrey remained entranced. 'Doesn't the sand get in and irritate him?'

" 'No . . . er, well, maybe it does, but if there's no need for the hole, then it will disappear in the process of evolution. Now I am passing out these sheets and for the rest of the period you are expected to do independent research based on my questions.' Silently, the children went to work.

"I went home, stunned by what I had seen. Thoughts ran through my head. No one had smiled. In the whole time, no one had smiled. . . . No teacher showed delight in children. No teacher had bothered to motivate. Motivation is not just a procedural item taught in teacher's college. . . . It is the process that prepares a child for loving. All that we call education was conceived in love. It was because man so loved the shell that he gave it a name. It was his way of getting closer to it, paying homage to it, of summoning it up in his thoughts even when the creature itself was absent. The act of naming is the act of loving—be it a decimal point, a part of speech,

or a shell. And the act of loving requires preparation—warmth, caring, ease, sensitivity, tenderness,
skill. What I had witnessed had nothing of this. It
was more like a sadistic attempt at forcible penetra-
tion—a raping of children. And still we demand that
the children respond. There is only one proper response to rape. For a woman it is the closing of her
legs; for a child, the closing of his mind."

IS THERE HOPE?

The sad fact is that the incidents in this chapter are not unusual. They occur daily in thousands
of classrooms all over the nation. Can these teachers
change?

There is a story about an oriental king who
bought a portrait of Moses. His advisers examined
the picture and concluded that Moses was cruel,
greedy, and selfish. The king was puzzled because
Moses was known as a kind, generous, and coura-
geous leader. The king decided to visit Moses in
person. After getting to know him, the king said,
"My advisers were wrong. They misjudged you
completely." But Moses disagreed. "They saw what
I was made of," he explained. "But they could not
see my struggle against it. Thus, they missed knowing what I became."

Improvement seldom occurs spontaneously. More often it is attained by deliberate effort. Every teacher can become aware of attitudes that alienate, words that insult, and acts that hurt. He can acquire competence and caution in communication, and become less abrasive and less provocative.

James Joyce said, "History is a nightmare from which I am trying to wake up." To some extent, every person's history holds terrors from which he needs to wake up: invisible rules, irrational restrictions, and harmful beliefs. A teacher cannot hold on to unexamined taboos, to prejudices that paralyze, and to feelings that freeze. To see the world through children's eyes, a teacher needs infinite emotional flexibility. The chronological distance and psychological chasm that separates children from adults can be bridged only by genuine empathy—the capacity to respond accurately to a child's needs, without being infected by them.

The temper of our time encourages aggression; belligerence masquerades as power, and confrontation as justice. Civility is often mistaken for servility. Teachers are confronted with increasing brashness of children. Yet they cannot afford to "do unto others as is done unto them." Learning depends on the emotional climate engendered by empathy and civility. In their daily contacts with children, teachers must preserve these vanishing virtues.

That the results justify the effort is illustrated by the following tale:

A bossy man decided to change his behavior toward his cook. He called him in and said: "From now on I'm going to be nice to you."

"If I'm a little late with lunch you won't yell at me?" asked the cook.

"No," said the boss.

"If the coffee is a little cold you won't throw it in my face?" asked the cook.

"No," said the boss.

"If the steak is too well done, you won't deduct its cost from my salary?" asked the cook.

"Definitely not," assured the boss.

"Okay," said the cook. "Then I'll stop spitting in your soup."

Children have so many opportunities to spit in our educational soup, it is in our interest to reduce their wish for revenge.

No one denies the need for change in school structure and course content. But, as this chapter illustrates, many problems of education are rooted in teacher-student *relations*. For any school reform to have an effect, these must change.

Congruent Communication*

*Communication that is harmonious, authentic; where words fit feelings.

Where do we start if we are to improve life in the classroom? By examining how we respond to children. How a teacher communicates is of decisive importance. It affects a child's life for good or for bad. Usually we are not overly concerned about whether our response conveys acceptance or rejection. Yet to a child this difference is fateful, if not fatal.

Teachers who want to improve relations with children need to unlearn their habitual language of rejection and acquire a new language of acceptance. To reach a child's mind a teacher must capture his heart. Only if a child feels right can he think right.

SANE MESSAGES

What counts most in adult-child communication is the *quality* of the process. A child is entitled to sane messages from an adult. How parents and teachers talk tells a child how they feel about him. Their statements affect his self-esteem and self-worth. To a large extent, their language determines his destiny.

Parents and teachers need to eradicate the insanities so insidiously hidden in their everyday speech, the messages that tell a child to distrust his perception, disown his feelings, and doubt his worth. The prevalent, so-called "normal," talk drives children crazy—the blaming and shaming, preaching and moralizing, ordering and bossing, admonishing and accusing, ridiculing and belittling, threatening and bribing, diagnosing and prognosing. These techniques brutalize, vulgarize, and dehumanize children. Sanity depends on trusting one's inner reality. Such trust is engendered by processes that can be identified and applied. The various methods of communication suggested in this chapter describe processes conducive to driving children sane.

THE CARDINAL PRINCIPLE

Chapters Two and Three contain episodes illustrating teachers at their best and at their worst. Is there one principle of communication which "teachers at their best" observe and "teachers at their worst" violate?

At their best, teachers address themselves to a child's situation. At their worst, they judge his character and personality. This, in essence, is the difference between effective and ineffective communication.

1. A child forgot to return a book to the library. Addressing himself to the situation, Teacher A said, "Your book needs to be returned to the library. It's overdue." Addressing himself to the child's character, Teacher B said, "You are so irresponsible! You always procrastinate and forget. Why didn't you return the book to the library?"

2. A child spilled paint. Addressing himself to the situation, Teacher A said, "Oh. I see the paint spilled. We need water and a rag." Addressing himself to the child's character, Teacher B said, "You are so clumsy. Why are you so careless?"

3. A teenager has been coming to school disheveled, hair unkempt and clothes wrinkled. Addressing himself to the situation, Teacher A said, "Improvement is definitely needed in your grooming and attire." Addressing himself to the teenager's character, Teacher B said, "Everything about you is a mess. Your clothes are disheveled. Your hair is dirty. Even your brain is disorganized. What's the matter with you? Unless you shape up, you'll be thrown out of this class."

4. A child failed Spanish. Teacher A talked about the situation: "I am concerned about your

work in Spanish. It needs improvement. Can I be of help?" Teacher B talked about the child's character and personality: "You are a bright boy. You're intelligent. How come you failed? You'd better buckle down to work."

In all of the preceding situations, Teacher A conveyed concern and caring. Teacher B aroused anxiety and resentment. One was solution-oriented, the other problem-creating.

"Talk to the situation, not to the personality and character" is the cardinal principle of communication. It holds true for all encounters between teacher and child. Knowing how to apply this principle under varied conditions is the essence of effective communication.

Translated into classroom procedures, this principle would change a teacher's basic approach to children—his expression of anger and the tenor of his commands, his method of criticism and style of praise, his system of evaluating and categories of grading, his ways of comforting and means of reassuring, his routine of testing and manner of speaking.

EXPRESSING ANGER

I once asked a group of five hundred teachers if they remembered any lecture in teachers college that told them: "Children will often irritate you, annoy you, and make you angry. This is what you can do when angry."

None of the teachers had had such instruction.

One teacher replied: "The fact that no one acknowledged the problem told us a great deal. It told us that a good teacher never gets angry."

I then asked: "How many of you don't get angry, at least once a day?" No one raised his hand. All of them knew anger. Many confessed feeling guilty about being angry. Some felt unfit for their calling because of the anger children provoked in them.

The realities of teaching—the overloaded classes, the endless demands, the sudden crises—make anger inevitable. Teachers need not apologize for their angry feelings. An effective teacher is neither a masochist nor a martyr. He does not play the role of a saint or act the part of an angel. He is aware of his human feelings and respects them. Though he cannot always be patient, he is always authentic. His response is genuine. His words fit his feelings. He does not hide his annoyance. He does not pretend patience. He does not demonstrate hypocrisy by acting nice when feeling nasty.

An enlightened teacher is not afraid of his anger, because he has learned to express it without doing damage. He has mastered the secret of expressing anger without insult. Even under provocation he does not call children abusive names. He does not attack their character or offend their personality. He does not tell them whom they resemble and where they will end up. When angry, an enlightened teacher remains real. He describes what he sees, what he feels, and what he expects. He attacks the problem, not the person. He knows that when angry, he is dealing with more elements than he can control. He protects himself and safeguards his students by using "I" messages.

"I am annoyed," "I am appalled," "I am furious" are safer statements than *"You* are a pest," "Look what *you* have done," *"You* are so stupid," "Who do *you* think *you* are?"

When Mr. Hunt, the fourth-grade teacher, saw his classroom in disarray, he said, "I see books scattered all over the floor. I am displeased and angry. Books do not belong on the floor. They belong in your desks." The teacher deliberately avoided insult ("You are such slobs! You mess up everything in this class. You are so irresponsible."). A fifth-grade class was rambunctious. The teacher consciously avoided insult and attack ("You are like wild animals."). Instead, he stated firmly, "I get incensed when exposed to high-decibel behavior." The noise subsided. The discussion focused on the meaning of the statement.

When Mrs. Brooks, the kindergarten teacher, saw five-year-old Alan throw a stone at his friend, she said loudly, "I saw it. I am indignant and dismayed. Stones are not for throwing at people. People are not for hurting."

The teacher intentionally avoided insult and shame:

"Are you crazy?"

"You could have injured your friend."

"You could have crippled him. Is that what you want?"

"You are a cruel child."

Two boys made bullets out of bread and threw them at each other. They messed up the room. "I get angry when I see bread made into bullets," said the teacher. "Bread is not for throwing. This room needs immediate cleaning." Without a word the boys cleaned up the room. This teacher deliberately avoided attack and insult. He did not say, "You two slobs! Clean it up now! You are not fit to live in a pigsty. I want to talk to your parents about your disgusting behavior!"

The class was getting ready to go to the gym. Two girls started playing catch with their sneakers. The teacher's first impulse was to yell and punish. She stopped herself and said, "It makes me angry to see that. Sneakers are not for throwing. They are for wearing in gym." The throwing stopped and the girls went to gym.

During a cleanup period in kindergarten, the teacher was helping the children to put away their blocks. Dora left her pile untouched and refused to help.

"Dora, there are still some blocks to be put away," said the teacher.

"I don't have to put them away if I don't want to," Dora replied.

"The rule is that blocks are to be removed during cleanup," the teacher said firmly.

"You clean them up," answered Dora. "I won't do it."

"Now I'm angry," said the teacher sternly. "I think we'd better terminate this conversation."

Crying, Dora said: "Please, Teacher, don't 'terbidate' the conversation. I'll remove the blocks."

"I'd appreciate it," the teacher responded as Dora went to work.

The teacher was firm and effective. She stated her demand without hesitation and insisted on it without insult. Neither did she indulge in lengthy explanations. Instead, she expressed her feelings and clarified her expectations.

When teachers are angry, children are attentive. They listen to what is said. Teachers have a unique opportunity to demonstrate good English. They can use their rich supply of English expressions to give vent to all nuances of anger: They can be uncomfortable, displeased, annoyed, irked, irritated, frustrated, aggravated, exasperated, livid, provoked, incensed, indignant, aghast, irate, angry, mad, furious, and enraged. They can be full of consternation, ire, and acrimony.

There are many more expressions of anger. Learning to use them is not easy, for the native tongue of lost tempers is insult. Yet, the salvation of communication between teacher and child depends on learning to express nuances of anger without nuances of insult. In learning this new method, teachers have a head start. Style flows from attitudes. Most teachers have the right attitudes and concern for children. All they need is a style of communication that demonstrates this concern. Every teacher can develop an aversion to words that humiliate, acts that pain, and gestures that degrade. Even when enraged, a teacher can avoid the dictionary of denigration. These self-imposed restraints do not bring blandness of expression. On the contrary, they enhance a teacher's style. He learns to rely on a different tongue, one that voices anger vividly, fearlessly, and harmlessly. A teacher's motto is: Indignation— yes! Indignity—no!

As one teacher put it: "Even in anger, I don't yield to sadism. I say to myself: You can make no gains now, but you can minimize losses! Make sure that inevitable ruptures are not irreparable."

Some teachers say, "Life is hard and full of insult. We must prepare children to cope with it by giving them a taste of insult in school." It is true that modern life is often like a rat race. People struggle to be first in line; they push, wrestle, insult, and lie.

Do we want to prepare children for such life? No. On the contrary. We need to tell children that rat races are not good for people. We want school to be not a replica of, but an alternative to, raw reality. Such a school needs teachers with sophisticated sensitivity and effortless empathy.

The creed fit for a teacher was best expressed by E. M. Forster: "I believe in aristocracy . . . not an aristocracy of power, based upon rank and influence, but an aristocracy of the sensitive, the considerate, and the plucky. Its members are to be found in all nations and classes. . . . They represent the true human tradition, the one permanent victory . . . over cruelty and chaos."*

INVITING COOPERATION

An enlightened teacher does not look at children as his natural friends. He sees them as complex human beings, capable of hating, loving, and feeling

* E. M. Forster, "What I Believe," in *Two Cheers for Democracy* (New York: Harcourt, Brace and Company, 1951).

ambivalent. Children are dependent on their teachers, and dependency breeds hostility. To reduce hostility a teacher deliberately provides children with opportunities to experience independence. The more autonomy, the less enmity; the more self-dependence, the less resentment of others.

One method of diminishing hostility is to give children a voice and a choice in matters that affect life in school. As one teacher testified, "Once I accepted the principle of respecting autonomy, I found many ways of applying it in the classroom. Here are two examples:

"It started to snow. The children ran to the window and began to scream and cheer. I offered them a choice: 'You can watch the snow in silence. You can go back to your work. You decide.' The noise died instantly. The children watched the snow in delightful calm.

"In assigning homework, I gave the class a choice of doing ten or fifteen arithmetic problems. Mark, age ten, exclaimed, 'I can't do anything extra!' 'Do the number you feel is best for you,' I answered. 'I guess it won't hurt me to do the fifteen problems,' replied Mark."

Avoiding commands is another effective method of decreasing defiance. Like adults, children hate to be ordered around, dictated to, and bossed ("Do what you are told! Don't ask questions!"). They resent infringements on autonomy. They resist a teacher less when his communications convey respect and safeguard self-esteem. Examples:

TEACHER A: The noise is annoying.
TEACHER B: Stop that noise.

TEACHER A: The arithmetic assignment is on page sixty.
TEACHER B: Take out your arithmetic books and open to page sixty.

TEACHER A: Your book is on the floor. (*Next statement if needed:* "It belongs on the desk.")
TEACHER B: Pick up your book.

TEACHER A: The door is open. (*Next statement if needed:* "It has to be closed.")
TEACHER B: Close the door!

Teacher B tells children what to do. Teacher A avoids giving orders. He merely describes the situation. What needs to be done becomes obvious in the context. It is the child's conclusion, not the adult's command. Self-inferred decisions decrease defiance, reduce resistance, and invite collaboration.

Granting in fantasy what cannot be given in reality is another effective method of gaining cooperation.

A group of children surrounded the teacher's desk while she was doing clerical work. They bombarded her with questions, until she felt annoyed. Usually she would have said, "Don't bother me.

Don't you see I'm busy?" This time she turned to each child and said, "I *wish* I had the time to listen to you." The individual attention and the words "I wish" seemed to help the children bear their frustration. Instead of walking away grumbling, they returned to their seats quietly.

A fourth-grade teacher read a story to her class entitled *Five Chinese Brothers*. Each child had to draw his impression of them. The children ran up to the desk, holding up their drawings and vying loudly for attention. The teacher's first impulse was to yell, "Sit down. I don't have two hundred eyes. Don't get out of your seats. Don't call out my name," etc. Instead she said, "I *wish* I could see all your drawings at once. Perhaps you can help each other. Discuss your ideas with your neighbor, while I walk around and make suggestions." The children quieted down. The only noise heard was of excited whispers. Teamwork triumphed.

The teacher won the children's cooperation graciously. She avoided giving orders. She granted symbolically what she could not give in reality and encouraged self-reliance and teamwork.

Some teachers invite resistance and misbehavior by fragmenting and multiplying their demands. Here is an example, video-taped in a classroom by Jacob S. Kounin.

"The teacher was making a transition from spelling to arithmetic lessons as follows:

1. All right, everybody, I want you to close your spelling books.
2. Put away your red pencils.
3. Now close your spelling books.
4. Put your spelling books in your desk.
5. Keep them out of the way.
6. Take out your arithmetic books and put them on your desks in front of you.
7. That's right, let's keep everything off your desks except your arithmetic books.
8. And let's sit up straight. We don't want lazybones, do we?
9. That's fine. Now get your black pencils.
10. Open your books to page sixteen."*

The ten commands were unnecessary and unhelpful. They engendered resentment and slowed down learning. A succinct announcement, "Now it's time for arithmetic; the assignment is on page sixteen," would have given children greater autonomy and invited greater cooperation.

Said one teacher: "I deliberately avoid provoking defensive responses in the classroom. My communications omit pressure phrases: 'You must . . .' 'You had better . . .' I want to win cooperation with-

---

* Jacob S. Kounin, *Discipline and Group Management in Classrooms*, p. 106. Numbers not in the original; added here for emphasis. See bibliography, page 319.

out resorting to guilt and fear. I resist the temptation to turn requests and demands into moralistic judgments."

Another teacher said: "I've given up polemics in the classroom. My arguments only brought counterarguments to justify defiance and postpone compliance. It is easier to gain cooperation by changing moods than by changing minds."

ACCEPTANCE AND ACKNOWLEDGMENT

Teachers are told that children need understanding and acceptance. What they are not told is how to convey it under difficult classroom conditions. Communicating acceptance and understanding is a complex art with a unique language. Here are some guidelines:

In communicating with children there is a crucial difference between critical and uncritical messages. In making demands on children an uncritical message invites cooperation, a critical one engenders resistance. Examples:

A child interrupts his teacher.

TEACHER A: I would like to finish my statement.

TEACHER B: You are very rude. You are interrupting.

Two boys are conversing while homework is being assigned.

TEACHER A: I am assigning homework now. It needs to be written down.

TEACHER B: Don't you have anything better to do than to talk? Why don't you start writing this down?

Scene: *Monday morning. Class is in disorder. Children walk around, talking noisily.*

TEACHER A: I would like to begin.

TEACHER B: Stop the noise. Sit down. All of you. The weekend is over. This is not a discotheque.

A boy answers a teacher's questions without raising his hand or waiting his turn.

TEACHER A: I would like to hear answers from many children.

TEACHER B: Who gave you permission to talk? You are not the only one in the class. Stop monopolizing the discussion. It's rude and unfair.

In the preceding examples Teacher A's messages spared feelings and de-escalated conflict. Teacher B's messages aroused resentment and increased tension. To avoid critical messages, Teacher A stated what he felt and expected. He started his sentences with the word "I." Statements starting with the word "You" are best used in responding to the *child's* plight, complaint, or request.

The effective "you" message has the following qualities:

It accurately acknowledges the child's statement or state of mind.
It does not deny his perception.
It does not dispute his feelings.
It does not disown his wishes.
It does not deride his taste.
It does not denigrate his opinions.
It does not derogate his character.
It does not degrade his person.
It does not argue with his experience.

Six-year-old Arnold told his teacher that he saw a man taller than the Empire State Building. The teacher did not argue with Arnold's perception. She did not hurry to point out that no man can be so big. She did not tell him, "Stop lying, stop telling tall tales." Instead she acknowledged his perception with sympathy and humor. She asked the following questions: "You saw a tall man? A big man? A giant of a man? He was enormous? Tremendous looking? Bulky? Gigantic?" To each of these, Arnold answered, "Yes." "You saw a man who could be called big, tall, bulky, tremendous, enormous, and gigantic," summed up the teacher. Her lesson was good in human relations as well as in vocabulary.

Twelve-year-old Rae complained to her homeroom teacher that she had too much homework and an unfinished school assignment. The teacher deliberately did not argue with Rae's statement. She did not say: "Don't be ridiculous. When I was your age we had ten times as much homework. And as for the assignment, you have only yourself to blame. If you had finished it in class, you wouldn't have to do it at home. So stop complaining and start working or you'll fail."

The teacher acknowledged Rae's complaint factually and sympathetically: "You seem upset about the homework. It does seem like a lot of work for one day, especially with this unexpected school assignment. Mmmm." Rae felt understood and somewhat relieved. She said, "I'd better hurry home. I have lots of work to do."

During gym, one boy refused to jump into the pool. "The water is too cold," he cried, "and I don't feel so well." The teacher responded: "The water is fine. It is you who is all wet. The pool is heated, but you have cold feet. You are scared like a rabbit and cry like a little baby. You have a strong voice but a weak character."

This message denies the child's perception, argues with his experience, disputes his feelings, derogates his character, and degrades his person. A helpful "you" response acknowledges perception and does not argue with experience:

"You don't feel well and the water seems cold.

You wish you didn't have to jump in the pool today."

Such a response tends to diminish resistance. The child feels accepted and respected. His words are taken seriously, and he is not blamed.

After a pause the teacher can ask, "What do you suggest?" Thus, rather than supplying a ready-made solution, the teacher involves the child in finding an answer. Often when a teacher takes care of a child's feelings, the child gathers strength to cope with reality.

LABELING IS DISABLING

Simon, age fourteen, was late for school. His teacher said, "What's your excuse this time?" Simon told his story. The teacher answered, "I don't believe a word you said. I know why you are late: You are too lazy to get up on time. I still remember your brother; he too suffered from congenital indolence. If you don't shape up, you know where you'll end up."

In one minute, this teacher managed to violate several tenets of effective education. He diagnosed, labeled, and embarrassed a person in public. He offended him and his family and gave gloom warnings and doom predictions.

Recommendation: In dealing with students, avoid diagnosis and prognosis. Do not delve into the case history of the child or his family. Diagnosing children is dangerous. Labeling is disabling. The diagnosis may become the disease. A child often lives up to a teacher's negative prediction. He becomes what he is told he is.

To a child who is late, a teacher can state his expectations and feelings: "I don't like to stop and start in the middle of a lesson. Disruptions are annoying."

There is *no place* in education for the rich repertoire of familiar diagnostic and prognostic statements:

"You are such a crybaby, wise guy, dreamer, etc."

"You are so irresponsible, unreliable, incorrigible, etc."

"You are just looking for attention, for trouble, for sympathy, etc."

"Hello, Clown, Stupid, Genius, etc."

"You are all a bunch of sadists, fools, imbeciles, etc."

"You'll end up in the gutter, in jail, in prison, etc."

"You are a disgrace to school, family, country, etc."

Once teachers assimilate the principle of "no labeling," they become more helpful, even in difficult moments.

Phil, age ten, inadvertently bumped into a standing blackboard and toppled it over. Frightened, he stood frozen in his place. Usually, the teacher would have said, "What's the matter with you? You are so clumsy. Why are you so careless? And why are you standing like an idiot? What are you waiting for?"

This time the teacher's response was different. He followed an inner command: "Talk about the situation. Don't label the person." The teacher said, "These standing blackboards are a pain. One touch and they fall. Do you need any help?" Phil was taken aback by his teacher's unexpected response. He lifted the blackboard, picked up the chalk, and cleaned up the mess. His eyes told how grateful he was to his helpful teacher.

A wise teacher talks to children the way he does to visitors at his home. If his guest, Mrs. Smith, forgot her umbrella, he would not run after her shouting, "Scatterbrain! Every time you visit my home you forget something. If it's not one thing, it's another. You'd probably forget your head if it weren't attached to your shoulders. I want to live to see the day when you remember to be responsible for your own possessions. I am not your slave to pick up after you."

His comment would probably be, "Mrs. Smith, here is your umbrella." Yet the same teacher feels almost compelled to criticize a child who forgot his books or lunch box or glasses.

Another example:

If Mr. Brown, a guest at the teacher's home, stretched himself out, shoes on, on the living room couch, the teacher would not say, "Are you crazy? How dare you put your dirty shoes on my clean couch! You ruin everything in this house. Get your feet on the floor this instant. If I catch you doing it once more, just once more, I'll punish you. So help me. Mark my words."

What would the teacher tell his guest? He would probably say, "Mr. Brown, I am afraid that the couch will get dirty." A host deliberately does not tell his guests what to do. He has faith in their ability to figure it out, once his concern is brought to their attention.

Children often live up to what parents expect them to be, and what teachers tell them they are. It is damaging to tell a child where he will end up. Destinations may become destinies.

Doom predictions create psychological fissures in the lives of children. Like geological faults, they spell disaster. A teacher has awesome power to plant seeds of doubt in a child's mind about his fate. Example: Ernest, age sixteen, confided in his teacher his plan to become an archeologist. With obvious contempt the teacher said, "You an archeologist? You couldn't find a cuff link in a jewelry box, let alone a shard on a hillside."

Generations of children, especially minority children, have been convinced of their intellectual anemia by destructive persuasion. Many children leave school believing that their predestined fate precludes scholarship, enlightenment, or even happiness. This is tragedy. It is not the adult's role to impose upon children small dreams and imaginary limitations.

CORRECTION IS DIRECTION

Helpful correction is direction. It describes processes. It does not judge products or persons.

George, age fifteen, wrote an essay on the generation gap. His teacher did not like it. In red ink, he wrote, "Pretentious prose. Stuffy style. Loquacious and long-winded." George was hurt and discouraged. The biting evaluation killed his motivation. He hated himself and his teacher.

A high school English teacher criticized a student's short story as follows: "Cluttered and wordy. You write as though you had verbal diarrhea."

One teacher, an author of some note, wrote on a teenager's poem, "You have a tangential tongue.

You write a blue streak, but your words have a permanent overcast." The same teacher wrote on another child's composition: "You are an expert in the art of bad writing. You are charged with mutilating the King's English."

Children need guidance, not criticism. Instead of calling the prose "pretentious and loquacious," a concerned teacher shows how to write unpretentiously and succinctly. Example:

One teacher encouraged brevity by showing a verbose writer what to omit. The teacher wrote, "Avoid introductory phrases: 'The next point to be discussed,' 'It is necessary to bear in mind,' 'A significant fact to mention.' Start directly with your facts. The reader will know that it is the next point, and he will decide for himself whether it is significant and worth bearing in mind."

Another teacher advised students: "Get right to the point. State events and feelings directly. Avoid prefaces such as 'I would like to tell a story about' and 'I want to share a very important insight.' Instead, tell the story and share the insight."

To encourage succinct expression one teacher advised: "When possible do not start sentences with 'There are,' 'There is,' 'It is.' Begin with your subject. 'Views differ' is more effective than 'It is apparent that there are different views.' 'Use verbs instead of nouns: 'considered,' not 'took into consideration'; 'tended,' not 'had a tendency'; 'talked,' not 'engaged in verbal interchange.' "

To discourage verbosity one teacher said, "Make your writing lean. Look for words you can omit. When possible use a single word instead of a phrase: 'because,' not 'for the reason that'; 'while,' not 'during the time that'; 'since,' not 'owing to the fact that.'"

One teacher asked children to write a composition twice, once in simple and once in ponderous English. Thus they learned the difference between honest and pretentious prose.

To convince children of the need for clarity, one teacher pointed out the tragic result of garbled communication:

"[It is] death on the highway caused by a badly worded roadsign, heartbreak among lovers caused by a misplaced phrase in a well-intentioned letter, anguish of a traveler . . . not being met because of a slipshod telegram."*

On a confusing composition, the teacher wrote: "Rewrite, using a newspaper style. Tell your reader who, what, where, when, and why." The teacher related, "I resist the temptation to tear into a child and say, 'I can't make heads or tails of your paper. How could you have written such a confusing piece? You write like a moron.' But I know better. Tactless comments defeat a child. They do not improve his writing."

---

* William Strunk and E. B. White, *The Elements of Style.* (New York: The Macmillan Company, 1959), p. 65.

TEACHERS' QUESTIONS

Communication, like health, depends on acts of prevention. An enlightened teacher learns to omit messages that make a child feel foolish, guilty, enraged, and vengeful. He deliberately avoids questions and comments that are likely to incite resentment and invite resistance.

A teacher's question is not an abstraction to a child. It has concrete consequences for his life. A child experiences hostile inquiries as a rack on which his life is stretched out for painful scrutiny.

The following baker's dozen of destructive "whys" were asked by a fifth-grade teacher during one day of instruction:

1. Why can't you be good for a change?
2. Why are you so selfish?
3. Why do you have to fight with everybody?
4. Why can't you be like other children?
5. Why must you interrupt everybody?
6. Why can't you keep your mouth shut once in a while?
7. Why are you so slow?
8. Why do you always rush?
9. Why must you be such a pest?
10. Why are you so disorganized?
11. Why are you such a busybody?

12. Why do you forget everything I tell you?
13. Why are you so stupid?

Once upon a time, "why" was a term of inquiry. This meaning has long vanished. It was corrupted by the misuse of "why" as a coin of criticism. To children, "why" stands for disapproval, disappointment, and displeasure. It elicits echoes of past blame. Even a simple "Why did you do that?" may evoke the memory of "Why in the world did you ever do something as stupid as that?"

A wise teacher avoids harmful questions.

A child said: "I am not prepared for the test." The teacher resisted the temptation to ask why not. He knew that such a question would only provoke excuses, half-truths, and defensive lies. The teacher said, "We have a problem. What's the solution? What are your options?"

This nondramatic response has an indelible impact. It conveys respect, safeguards autonomy, and leaves with the child the responsibility for his life.

CHILDREN'S COMMENTS

Children often come up with questions or comments that seem unrelated to the topic under discussion. The class was studying railroads. One little girl said, "My grandmother was very sick." Teacher A: "And you went to visit her by railroad?" Teacher B: "Does your grandma have wheels? Is she a railroad? Why do you bring her into our discussion? You always manage to say something silly."

The class was studying protective coloration. One child said, "My dog bites anyone who touches her puppies." Teacher A: "You see a relation between protective coloration and protection of a puppy by its mother." Teacher B: "What does this have to do with our subject? Why don't you stick to the lesson?"

In the middle of a discussion on health, one little boy asked, "What happens to people after they die?" Teacher A: "You have raised an important question. Men have been wondering about that for thousands of years." Teacher B: "I don't know. I haven't asked them."

In each of these exchanges one teacher shows respect for the child, treats him as a person, and gives him credit for his question, even if it appears unrelated to the topic of the day. The other teacher attacks and insults. One educates; the other emasculates.

NO SARCASM

It is said that gentlemen never insult uninten-
tionally. Teachers sometimes do. They hurt children inadvertently. A teacher with an acid tongue
is a health hazard. His caustic comments deflate self-
esteem and block learning. Hurt children grow preoccupied with revenge fantasies.

The following remarks were made by teachers
nonchalantly, almost without awareness of their
tragic impact:

"You are relying on your own judgment again.
Believe me, it's a poor guide."

"Do you think you can come back to your
senses? You have been out of them quite a while."

"I have never seen so many 'geniuses' in one
room."

"Must you touch everything? What are you—
spastic?"

"Your intelligence is not good enough for this
class. Why don't you transfer to a school more com-
mensurate with your disabilities?"

"You don't need a psychologist; you need a
vacuum cleaner. Your mind is cluttered with junk."

CHILD: I had a severe headache last night and didn't
    study for the test. May I be excused for now
    and take the test another day?

TEACHER: O.K. But put "Mental Problem" on top of your test and a big zero on the bottom.

There is no place for devastating remarks in teacher-child communication. A professional teacher shuns comments that casually destroy a child's self-esteem. A teacher's role is to heal, not to injure. A teacher with a critical disposition and a gifted tongue has a grave responsibility: He must protect young children from his deadly talent, either by learning new ways of communicating or by choosing another calling.

NO HURRIED HELP

A modern teacher educates children to value their emotions. He helps them recognize and respect their inner feelings. Above all, he is cautious not to confuse children about how they feel. He does not tell an angry child, "You have nothing to be angry about," or a frightened child, "There is nothing to be afraid of." He does not advise a child in pain to smile, or a bashful child not to be shy. He does not tell his class, "Pretend you are happy when you are not."

When a child is told, "There is nothing to be afraid of," his fear increases. The child gets thrice frightened: In addition to his original fear, he is now afraid to be afraid and fearful that he will not be able to hide his fright. Fear does not vanish when banished. It does not disappear when its existence is not recognized. When a child is afraid, it is best to acknowledge his fear openly and with respect.

When ten-year-old Hope spoke of her fear of tests the teacher responded, "Tests can be scary, especially final exams." He intentionally avoided quick consolation: "It's not so terrible. If you have done your work, you have nothing to fear." Such a statement would push Hope into panic. Her inner response would be: "If I fail the exam, the teacher will think I didn't do my work."

A child comes to a teacher with a problem. The teacher wants to help. In fact, he has the solution ready. Yet he does not rush to offer it. He knows that children resist hasty help. They experience it as a threat to their intelligence. Retrospectively, it makes them feel stupid. "I must be dumb to have thought that I had such a difficult problem, when the solution is so simple. That I didn't figure it out myself only proves that I am stupid."

Neither is the child helped by quick reassurance:

"It's not such a big problem."
"You don't really have a problem."
"Everyone has such problems."

"It's a typical teenage worry."
"It's an easy problem to solve."
"Don't worry about it."

The teacher listens to the problem, rephrases it, clarifies it, gives the child credit for formulating it, and then asks, "What options are open to you?" "What are your choices in this situation?" Often the child himself comes up with a solution. Thus, he learns that he can rely on his own judgment. When a teacher hastily offers solutions, children miss the opportunity to acquire competence in problem-solving and confidence in themselves.

BREVITY

A story is told about a playwright who went to a psychiatrist for help. "I talk to myself," he complained. "Well," reassured the doctor, "lots of people talk to themselves." "But," protested the man, "you don't know what a bore I am." A teacher, like a playwright, has an obligation to be interesting or, at least, brief. A play closes when it ceases to interest audiences. Students close their minds to an over-talkative teacher. To be told "you talk like a teacher" is not a compliment. Why? Because teachers have the reputation of dwelling on a subject and overstating the obvious. This provokes a reaction in most listeners of "All right. That's enough already." The following three incidents were video-taped in ongoing classes by Jacob S. Kounin.

John lost his pencil. The teacher said:

1. "Did you find your pencil? . . .
2. I'd like to know what you did with it. . . .
3. Did you eat it? . . .
4. What happened to it?
5. What color was it?
6. You can't do your work without it."

The teacher then looked for a pencil, saying:

7. "I'll get you a pencil.
8. Make sure the pencil is here tomorrow morning.
9. And don't tell me you lost that one, too.
10. And make it a new one, and see that it's sharpened." *

These ten sentences were all unnecessary. The teacher could have handed John a pencil graciously, without saying a word, without preaching and probing, without wasting time, and without disturbing the class.

Every teacher needs to learn economical meth-

* Jacob S. Kounin, *Discipline and Group Management in Classrooms*, p. 104. Numbers not in the original. See bibliography, page 319.

ods of dealing with minor mishaps. A missing book, a broken pencil, a lost paper, or a forgotten assignment should not take up his time, effort, and energy. In all such situations a teacher remains solution-oriented. He aims to settle present problems without dwelling on future responsibilities and past philosophies. The following example illustrates dwelling on minor misbehavior.

1. "Richard, stop that talking. . . .
2. Some of you are cooperating and some of you aren't.
3. Mary is cooperating and doing her work and
4. so is Jimmy.
5. Mabel was not listening.
6. Now you all know this is not a playground.
7. This is a classroom and we're supposed to be learning.
8. Good citizens don't bother other children who are trying to learn, do they?
9. So let's all cooperate and be good citizens and not disturb other children.
10. It's hard to learn when there's a lot of noise." *

The teacher could have safely omitted the first

* Jacob S. Kounin, *Discipline and Group Management in Classrooms*, p. 102. Numbers not in the original. See bibliography, page 319.

nine of her ten statements. The last one might have sufficed to get the children's attention.

"The teacher is starting a lesson about telling time. . . . Margaret groaned softly. The teacher turned to Margaret and said:

1. 'Now, Margaret, did you come to school to learn? . . .
2. Is it so painful, Margaret? . . .
3. No, I don't think so.
4. Your parents are going to want you to tell time. . . .
5. And you're going to be very happy to learn telling time, Margaret.
6. You don't have to make all those groans because you don't want to tell time.
7. But after all, if your mother sees you can tell time you might get a watch of your own.' " *

None of these seven statements was helpful. They could all have been omitted. They only wasted time, and held back learning. Nagging does not motivate a child to learn how to tell time. It only makes him wish that class time passed faster. Instead of dwelling on Margaret's groan, the teacher could have responded with one sympathetic

* Jacob S. Kounin, *Discipline and Group Management in Classrooms*, p. 95. Numbers not in the original. See bibliography, page 319.

sentence: "I'll help you, Margaret." No long harangue was needed.

There is a story about a little girl who was asked how she liked her first day in school. She replied: "It was nice, except for one lady who kept interrupting." This sentiment is also expressed often by older students.

One high school girl said: "On a recent class trip, our teacher marred the view with explanations. He did not cease telling the exact heights of mountains and precise depths of valleys. He was passionate about the region's precipitation and spared us no speculation on how each rock had been formed. He destroyed all poetic vistas with his nonstop erudition."

Many teachers believe in the power of pontification. Yet ultimately, intellectual explanations fail to educate. As Saul Bellow put it: "Intellectual man has become an explaining creature. Fathers to children, wives to husbands . . . experts to laymen . . . doctors to patients, man to his own soul, explained. . . . For the most part, in one ear, out the other." *

Many modern children are reared on various misconceptions of Freudian theory and are fed explanations with their mother's milk. From early

* Saul Bellow, *Mr. Sammler's Planet* (New York: Viking, 1970).

infancy, they are overexposed to "analysis"; their personality is invaded, their motivation questioned, and their conduct explained. Such children become allergic to loquacious teachers.

How does a child come to terms with school's complex demands? Not by rules of reason. For children, learning is never without emotional overtones. Whenever a teacher ignores the emotions and resorts to long logical explanations, learning limps to a halt.

One principal advised a verbose teacher: "Talk like a reporter writes: headlines, main points, specific details. Look for brevity. Don't be known as a man of a few thousand words. Whenever possible, start at the end."

IMPACT ON CHILDREN

A teacher is often unaware of the impact of his words on the lives of children. Do enlightened methods of communication make a difference? Can children tell the difference between benign and destructive messages? Do they respond differently to them? The following statements by sixth-graders answer these questions:

"The same kids who are cooperative in Mrs. A.'s class go off like firecrackers in Mrs. B.'s class. The way a child behaves depends on the teacher.

For instance, when Herbert returned to school after a week of absence, Mrs. A. said, 'Welcome back, Herbie. We missed you.' Herb was glad and behaved well. Mrs. B. said, 'No wonder it was so quiet last week. Herb was out.' Herbert didn't stop making noise for the rest of the hour."

"There are a lot of things about teachers that I don't like. I hate their 'shoulds' and 'coulds.' For instance, Mr. J. says, 'Now by the end of the week, you *should* be able to play your piece well.' When I don't play it so well, he says, 'You *could* have done better if only you had practiced more.' I also resent it when he compares me to others. He says, 'I teach a little boy in the first grade, and he plays this piece easily.' Well, I'm not someone else. I'm me!"

"What really gets me is the way my teacher talks to some of the kids in the class. She keeps saying, 'Kelly, I give up. You'll never change.' How can he change if she keeps telling him he'll never change? Once she said, 'Tom, I'm surprised at you. That's the kind of behavior I'd expect from Kelly, not from you.' Get it? She hit both of us with one blow."

"I never ask Mrs. R. any questions, because I know her answer: 'That's a stupid question!' I once told her, 'There's no such thing as a stupid question. There's only a question that needs an answer!' She looked at me with contempt and said, 'That's a stupid statement.' You just can't win."

Jo, age twelve, expressed to her mother anger and disdain for her teacher.

MOTHER: You can't completely condemn your teacher. She has *some* redeeming qualities.

JO: Name one good thing she did.

MOTHER: Well, she produced a fine Columbus Day play. I saw it myself.

JO (*Scowls, points her finger and lets her voice become harsh*): You! David! You're going to be out of the play unless you know all of your lines by tomorrow. I'll get someone else to take your part. And I don't want to hear any excuses! I'm not interested in anything you have to say. Either you have your lines memorized by tomorrow or you're out! (*Changing back to her normal voice*) Oh yes. She produced a very good play.

"Funny about teachers. It's hard to think of them as people. Sometimes when you see them after school and they talk to you personally, you're sur-prised—because they talk like human beings. But in class they walk around like robots, waiting for you to do something bad so they can yell at you. Except for Mrs. D. . . . She is a person even when she is a teacher."

CONGRUENT COMMUNICATION

Congruent communication can transform education. It strikes not just at the trappings of teaching, but at the heart of learning. Yet it has not been tried in our schools. Never has its full force been lavished on children to enrich their personalities and ennoble their lives.

Unlike pilots, architects, or surgeons, teachers are not rigorously trained in the skills of their calling. Somehow they are expected to enter the classroom well versed in the intricacies of human relations. In the course of their daily work teachers are called upon to

> motivate learning
> encourage autonomy
> bolster self-esteem
> engender self-confidence
> allay anxiety
> diminish fear
> decrease frustration
> defuse rage
> de-escalate conflict

Teachers, like parents, need a high degree of competence in communication. An enlightened teacher shows sensitivity to semantics. He knows that the substance learned by a child often depends on the style used by the teacher. He has an awareness of feelings and a fitting language to convey understanding. He is allergic to communication that changes children for the worse. He avoids blaming and shaming and is averse to insult and intimidation. His language is free of destructive dialogue and rhetorical rape.

Congruent communication is an achievement. It requires learning and rehearsing and self-discipline. It is not just "doing what comes naturally." Like all skill, it demands practice. Like all art, it requires selection. It is consoling, but untrue, to claim that in a good relationship one can say anything with impunity. It is like believing that when in good health one can swallow anything without harm— including poison.

One caution: A teacher cannot be artificial and effective. Nothing defeats him more than phoniness. No one can pretend respect and care without being detected. Skill divorced from genuineness is soon unmasked. In teacher-child relations there is no alternative to congruence.

CHAPTER 5

The Perils
of Praise

Evaluation or Appreciation?
The Process of Praise.
Implications of Evaluations.
Adjectives and Persons.
Praise and Misbehavior. Praise and Status.
Praise and Motivation. Creative Praise:
"Captivating Plot"; "Exotic Setting";
"Candidate for P.E.N.";
"Fit for *The New York Times*";
"Saga of a People"; Catching the Mood;
"Essence of Imperialism";
"Songs of Goliards"; "Talent for Topiary";
A Budding Actor; "Carnegie Hall."
Literary Language.

EVALUATION OR APPRECIATION?

True or false:
Praise is destructive.
Praise is productive.

Both statements are true. Evaluative praise is destructive. Appreciative praise is productive.

In psychotherapy a child is never told, "You are a good little boy." "You are doing great." "Carry on your good work." Judgmental praise is avoided. Why? Because it is not helpful. It creates anxiety, invites dependency, and evokes defensiveness. It is not conducive to self-reliance, self-direction, and self-control. These qualities demand freedom from outside judgment. They require reliance on inner motivation and evaluation. To be himself, one needs to be free from the pressure of evaluative praise.

If such praise is unhelpful, why is it sought? One may as well ask: If drugs are harmful, why are they craved? The answer to both questions is the same: Praise, like a drug, may make a child feel good—for the moment. However, it creates dependence. Others become his source of approval. He relies on them to quench his craving and establish his value. They must tell him his daily worth.

THE PROCESS OF PRAISE

Praise consists of two parts: What we say to the child and what he in turn says to himself. Our words should state what we like and appreciate about his efforts, help, work, and accomplishments. The child then draws conclusions about himself. When our statements describe the events and feelings realistically and appreciatively, the child's conclusions about himself are positive and productive.

Marcia, age twelve, helped the teacher rearrange the books in the class library. The teacher avoided personal praise ("You did a good job. You are a hard worker. You are a good librarian."). Instead she described what Marcia accomplished: "The books are all in order now. It'll be easy for the children to find any book they want. It was a difficult job. But you did it. Thank you." The teacher's words of recognition allowed Marcia to make her own inference. "My teacher likes the job I did. I am a good worker."

Phyllis, age ten, wrote a poem describing her reaction to the first snow of the season. The teacher said, "Your poem reflected my own feelings; I was delighted to see my winter thoughts put into such poetic phrases." A smile crossed the little poet's face. She turned to her friend and said, "Mrs. A. really *likes* my poem. She thinks I am terrific."

Ruben, age seven, had been struggling to make his handwriting neat. He found it difficult to keep his letters on the line. Finally, he managed to create a neat page with well-constructed letters. The teacher wrote on his paper: "The letters are neat. It was a pleasure to read your page." When the papers were returned, the children eagerly read the notes the teacher had written. Suddenly, the teacher heard the smacking of lips: There was Ruben *kissing* his paper! "I am a good writer," he announced.

EMILY (*age eleven*): How do you like my guitar playing?

TEACHER: That piece you just played had life to it. It sounded as if you really enjoyed it.

EMILY: I did. It's one of my favorites.

TEACHER: I can spot the ones you like. I can hear it in the sound. There is a little extra something that comes through.

EMILY: Do you think it's the way I feel about the music?

TEACHER: That could be it!

Since that conversation, Emily's appreciation of her own playing has increased. She plays with zest and takes pleasure in repeating favorite passages. In this episode, the teacher intentionally abstained from personal praise ("You are a great guitarist."). Instead she conveyed to Emily trust in her feelings. Emily herself concluded that she could rely on her own musical sense.

IMPLICATIONS OF EVALUATIONS

Positive evaluations may have negative implications. Judgmental praise may create anxiety and distance between people. It may constrict communication and terminate relations.

Andrea lost a five-dollar bill. Richard, age twelve, found it and handed it to the teacher. The teacher said, "You are a very honest boy. I am proud of you." Richard blushed. The teacher's words threw him into panic. Richard had a history of petty thievery. When the teacher praised him for his honesty, he was engulfed by anxiety. He thought: "If the teacher only knew . . ."

Richard withdrew into himself, fearful of contact with the teacher. He said to himself, "I must not let the teacher know me better. If he did, he would not be proud of me. He would be ashamed of me."

Richard's teacher would have been more helpful had he used appreciative praise: "Thank you, Richard, for finding the money. You saved Andrea much sorrow." Richard would have been delighted.

Conclusion: In praising appreciate specific acts. Do not evaluate character traits.

ADJECTIVES AND PERSONS

The young teacher wanted to encourage abstract thinking in her classroom. She showed an apple to Alice and asked, "What family does it belong to?" Alice blushed but did not know the answer. The teacher turned to Carol, who replied instantly, "Apple is in the fruit family." "Good girl, good girl," praised the teacher.

The teacher continued with her lesson, unaware of the damage she had done. If Carol is a good girl for knowing the answer, what does it make Alice for not knowing?—a bad girl.

In a democracy, one is not good for knowing

a fact or bad for not knowing it. One may know many facts and be a crook. Knowledge does not make one good. The lack of it does not make one bad.

The teacher could have supplied the missing answer to Alice, or confirmed the reply to Carol ("Apple is in the fruit family."). No evaluation of her person was necessary.

Conclusion: Avoid praise that attaches adjectives to a child's character.

PRAISE AND MISBEHAVIOR

It was Jim's birthday. Ten five-year-old boys and girls had snacks, played games, and sang *Happy Birthday* to Jim. All was well. The kindergarten teacher was delighted by the children's conduct and decided they deserved praise. She said: "My, my. What a wonderful bunch of boys and girls we have here. You behave like real angels."

A moment later, a fight broke out. Candies became bullets, cookies turned into torpedoes, cupcakes flew like guided missiles. The party was a bomb. The teacher was shocked. What burned her up most was that she had praised the children so sincerely. "Isn't praise good for children any more?" she asked bitterly.

When a child feels he does not deserve praise, he may misbehave to set the adult straight. The children at Jim's party did not see themselves as angels. When they were so labeled, they corrected the false image. They effectively dispelled their teacher's illusion.

Conclusion: Evaluative praise of conduct is undesirable. It may convey that we are surprised at "good" behavior because we expected misbehavior. Children often live up to our inferred expectation.

On a similar occasion another teacher, in contrast, said: "It was a pleasure to have this party in our kindergarten. Thank you for making it such fun." The children beamed. This teacher did not praise the children judgmentally. She only expressed her feelings of enjoyment and appreciation. The children themselves concluded that they were welcome and valued.

PRAISE AND STATUS

Praising is arrogating status. The praiser becomes the appraiser. He climbs into the seat of judgment and claims special competence. A young teacher presented an idea to an older colleague. She was met with the put-down statement, "That's a fine thought, young lady." The praise clearly apprised the young teacher of her place in the pecking order. Evaluative praise serves to put people of "lower status" in their place. Thus, it would be considered impertinent for a child to praise his teacher ("You are doing a good job, Teacher. You are top-notch. I am proud of you. Carry on your great work.").

If we met Picasso, we would not say to him, "You are a great painter. You are doing a fine job." We would not say to Leonard Bernstein, "You are a great musician, Mr. B., one of the best." We would sense that such evaluative praise is arrogant and in bad taste. We would not dare to set ourselves up as judges. We might say, "Thank you, Mr. Picasso, for your paintings. They have enriched my life." "Thank you, Mr. Bernstein, for your music. Your *West Side Story* brought me so much joy and your *Jeremiah Symphony* touched me deeply." Children deserve similar courtesy. They too need praise that appreciates, not praise that compares or condescends.

PRAISE AND MOTIVATION

Evaluative praise is often experienced as a threat. It brings discomfort, not delight; fear, not joy. Children often squirm under the stress of judgmental praise, and they become defensive and evasive. They sense that such praise intends to change them. They resent the intent and defy the manipulation.

Lori, age thirteen, played an impressionistic piece of music beautifully. The teacher was impressed by the eloquence of the performance.

TEACHER: Um . . . I enjoyed that very much.

LORI: I'm glad you didn't say that I played it "beautifully." Every time I play a piece, Mother gushes, "Beautiful, beautiful, beautiful. You put so much feeling into the music." I feel like I'm being bopped on the head.

TEACHER: You don't like an evaluation each time.

LORI: No, I don't need to be told how beautifully I play. I basically play the piano for myself. I'm not performing, so I don't want to be judged all the time.

Ben, age twelve, threw a dart at a target and hit the bull's-eye. His gym teacher said: "You are great. You have a perfect eye. You are a marksman." Ben walked away from the game. The teacher was surprised. He had intended to encourage him, but the praise apparently discouraged him. The teacher wondered why.

After the praise, Ben thought: "This teacher will expect my every dart to hit the bull's-eye. I am not a marksman. I scored by chance. If I try once more, I may not even hit the target, let alone the bull's-eye. I'd better quit while I'm ahead."

What kind of praise would have motivated Ben to continue his efforts? Non-judgmental, descriptive praise. The teacher might have said: "I see this dart hit the bull's-eye." Ben's inner response would have been: "The teacher does not expect every dart to hit the mark. It is safe to try again." If Ben's next dart had missed the bull's-eye, the teacher could have commented that the dart went to the right, or left, or up or down. From this objective statement about his performance Ben might have learned how to improve. But more important, Ben might have learned that the teacher's attitude toward him as a person did not depend on how well or badly he threw darts. In contrast, if a teacher's statements are evaluative ("You are good. You are great. You are an expert."), the child, when he misses the mark, may say to himself, "I am bad. I am terrible. I am a failure."

Conclusion: Only praise that does not judge the child's character or evaluate his personality makes it safe for him to err without fear and to recover without anxiety.

Six-year-old Don showed his teacher a drawing and said, "Doesn't it look sloppy?" The teacher looked at Don's art and said with sympathy, "It didn't come out the way you wanted it to. You are disappointed." Without a word, Don went to his desk and drew another picture. Then he asked his teacher: "How do you like this one?" The teacher answered: "I see you used many colors—red and black, and green and yellow." "And orange," corrected Don. "Yes," said the teacher. "Orange, too. It is such a colorful picture. I like it." Don beamed with joy. "I love colors," he confided. "They cheer me up." He went back to his desk to draw still another picture.

The teacher was helpful because she avoided evaluative statements. When Don showed her his first drawing, she did not say, "It's a sloppy picture." Instead, she described *his* feelings of disappointment. When Don showed her the second drawing, she did not say, "Oh, it's beautiful. You are such a good painter." Instead she described *her* feelings and *his* colors. Don was pleased, encouraged, and motivated to draw again.

Conclusion: Productive praise recognizes a child's feelings and describes his performance.

Olga, age nine, showed her teacher a blue painting. It was shapeless. The teacher knew how to respond constructively. She looked at it and said: "It's so blue." "Yes," answered Olga. The teacher looked again and said, "I see here it's light blue and here it's dark blue." "That's right," said Olga joyfully. "This is the sky and this is the sea." "Oh-h-h, I see," replied the teacher in a tone full of appreciation. "You made a seascape and a sky- scape." "Yes," agreed Olga. "I like to make seascapes and skyscapes—and landscapes too," volunteered Olga, as she started another painting.

The teacher did not ask Olga what the painting was supposed to be. Nor did she give it phony praise such as: "What a beautiful painting." Instead she described the painting and her feelings about it. As a result, Olga felt that her creativity was genuinely valued.

Orlando, age five, helped his kindergarten teacher clean up the lawn. From time to time the teacher praised him, helpfully: "I see you have a big pile of leaves. . . . You have two piles of leaves. . . . Don't tell me you have another pile already! . . . Five piles in one hour—that's what I call work. . . . I appreciate your help very much."

The teacher's words galvanized Orlando. He worked with energy and gusto. When his mother came to fetch him, he turned to his teacher and said, "Tell Mother about my piles of leaves."

The teacher did not praise Orlando by com- plimenting his personality or evaluating his char- acter. She did not say, "You are such a good boy. You are my little helper. What would I do without you?" She merely appreciated his efforts. Orlando himself concluded he had done a good job and was a great help.

Conclusion: Productive praise describes a child's efforts and accomplishments and our feelings about them. It does not evaluate personality or judge character. The cardinal rule in praising is: Describe without evaluating. Report—don't judge. Leave the evaluation of the child to him.

CREATIVE PRAISE

When teachers give up judgmental clichés (good, great, wonderful, excellent), they develop a vigorous and vivid language of appreciation and recognition. The following examples were supplied by the teachers in a special seminar on praise.

"CAPTIVATING PLOT"

Florence, age fifteen, wrote a play. Her teacher sent her a detailed note of praise: "Your dialogue is honed and crisp. Your plot is captivating, carefully constructed and paced. I liked your whole approach. It allowed your characters to erect their own scale of values by which to measure themselves." Florence was content beyond belief. Her teacher's words of praise not only recognized her talent but also supported her strivings for independence.

"Exotic Setting"

William, age sixteen, wrote a novella. The teacher praised it profusely and effectively. He wrote, "I liked your story. It is exotic in setting and fanciful in incident. You have unraveled your plot like a scenario; each scene is presented with precision." William felt motivated enough to contemplate another novel.

"Candidate for P.E.N."

Nancy, age fifteen, wrote a long and beautiful poem. Her teacher remarked: "Nancy, you are a candidate for P.E.N. International." "What's that?" asked Nancy. "The Association of Poets, Essayists, and Novelists," replied the teacher. Nancy beamed. She felt motivated to work and strive for this tempting goal.

"Fit for *The New York Times*"

Barbara, age fourteen, wrote an exhaustive report on racial tension in her school. Her teacher commented: "Barbara, your report is fit to be printed in *The New York Times*." This one sentence carried more incentive than a page full of personal praise.

"Saga of a People"

Jerome, age seventeen, wrote a long report on his visit to a collective settlement in Israel. The teacher praised it as follows:

"You have conveyed the trials and triumphs of the early pioneers. Reading your report I was able to visualize the sea of mud and the desert of dust being turned into gardens. You have movingly depicted the saga of a people."

Catching the Mood

Martin, age sixteen, wrote an essay on poverty in America. The teacher praised him as follows: "You sketched the scene and caught the mood of the poor in our country. I found your analysis incisive and your recommendations compelling."

"Essence of Imperialism"

Rodney, age eighteen, wrote an essay on the struggle of African nations for independence. The teacher praised him as follows: "In one sentence you have captured the essence of imperialism: 'economic exploitation backed by military power.'"

SONGS OF GOLIARDS

Enrico, age fifteen, wrote a series of earthy songs for his combo. His music teacher praised him, using terms calculated to enrich his cultural background. He said: "Your songs remind me of the music of the goliards."

"Goliards? Who are the goliards?" asked Enrico.

"Let's look it up in the encyclopedia," suggested the teacher.

Eagerly, Enrico found out that the goliards were the vagabond poets, vagrant scholars, and wandering monks—the hippies of the thirteenth century.

"TALENT FOR TOPIARY"

Chester, age sixteen, liked to work in the school's garden. He showed a special devotion in caring for flowers. The teacher praised him, using a difficult word. He said, "Chester, you have a talent for topiary."

"Topiary? What's that?" asked Chester.

"It is something worth looking up in the dictionary," said the teacher.

Chester was pleased to find out that he had talent in the "ancient art of pruning plants and trimming shrubs into geometrical shapes and animal forms."

A Budding Actor

Dahlia, age thirteen, was the main character in a comedy presented at the school auditorium. Her teacher wrote her the following note of praise: "It was a pleasure to watch you on stage. I found your characterization so funny my sides ached, because the laughs came so fast and furious."

"Carnegie Hall"

Leonard, age seventeen, conducted the school orchestra. His music teacher wrote him a note of praise: "You conducted the orchestra with dramatic intensity, showing decisive leadership and command of the music. I hope someday to see you conduct at Carnegie Hall."

LITERARY LANGUAGE

The following comments of praise by high school English teachers were deliberately phrased in literary language. The words were often new and difficult. But the teachers were sure that no student would fail to obtain the meaning of praise intended for him.

"You have a writer's sense of plot and place and

character. A work full of dramatic sense. Fun to read."

"Your essay on the hippie culture makes a convincing point for the validity of its own conventions."

"Your description of a person on the edge of madness is both clinically valid and dramatically alive."

"Your story affords sharp insights into men's struggle for a life of decency in a jungle of competition."

"Your prose is picturesque and your characters are believable. I enjoyed reading a story that was so vigorous and visual."

"Your illustrations match perfectly the spare elegance of the prose. They display gentleness and power, pain and hope."

"Your songs are written with moving simplicity —deep in feeling, rich in texture."

"Your descriptions of people and places are like pictures taken by a color camera: accurate, vivid, detailed."

"I noticed the workmanship, force, and precision reflected in your composition."

"Your poem conjures up images of power. A work of sensitivity and sense. Reading it is a reward in itself."

"Your report carries an intellectual ballast. No reader can miss the weight of its meaning."

"Your story mirrors the human condition. You managed to make the darkness visible."

"A murder mystery at its best. The menacing mood and perilous potential kept my interest from start to finish."

"Your dialogues are those of a playwright. They change with the characters—here funny, here frivolous; now solemn, now sardonic. A symphony of voices."

Descriptive praise in literary language tempts children to think and infer. Its residual ripples evoke echoes and compel conclusions which confront each child with his rightness. Such praise lodges itself firmly in the child's memory, strengthening his self-worth and enhancing his self-image.

CHAPTER 6

Discipline

Alternatives to Punishment. Self-Discipline.

Emphasis on Prevention. Note Passing.

"Who Put the Peels on My Desk?"

A Four-Letter Word. The Power of Poetry.

After the Fall. Laconic Language.

Long Words. Avoiding Trivia.

"To Be Sorry Is To Behave Differently."

A Verbal Attack. Angry Moments.

"I Can See How Angry You Are."

Exercises in Discipline. Fighting Pollution.

Encouraging Cooperation.

A Letter from the Teacher. To Save a Soul.

"Put It in Writing."

Dealing with Complaints.

A Face-Saving Exit. "Inside Voices."

Improve or Transfer. The Class as a Group:

"Withitness"; "Overlapping";

"Movement Management"; Group Focus;

A Personal Note.

To Side with the Hidden Asset.

ALTERNATIVES TO PUNISHMENT

A teacher was about to give his first lesson in a school for delinquent boys. He was very apprehensive. Success and failure hinged on this first meeting. As the teacher walked briskly to his desk, he stumbled and fell. The class roared in hilarious laughter. The teacher rose slowly, straightened up, and said, "This is my first lesson to you: A person can fall flat on his face and still rise up again." Silence descended. Then came applause. The message was received.

This teacher was a true disciplinarian. He used the force of wisdom to affect events. In a moment of distress he influenced children not with threats and punishment but with his power of personal response. His words touched on inner yearnings and turned disruption into contemplation.

The essence of discipline is finding effective alternatives to punishment. To punish a child is to enrage him and make him uneducable. He becomes a hostage of hostility, a captive of rancor, a prisoner of vengeance. Suffused with rage and absorbed in grudges, a child has no time or mind for studying. In discipline whatever generates hate must be avoided. Whatever creates self-esteem is to be fostered.

The most effective attitude toward discipline was summed up by an experienced teacher: "I assume that pupils come to school with a distorted self-image. I take for granted their precarious self-respect. Therefore, in dealing with children I am cautious. I am aware that my comments touch on inner feelings. I am sensitive not to lessen self-esteem. I am careful not to diminish self-worth."

Unlike ships, human relations founder on pebbles, not reefs. A teacher can be most destructive or most instructive in dealing with everyday disciplinary problems. His instant response makes the difference between condemnation and consolation, rage and peace. Good discipline is a series of little victories in which a teacher, through small decencies, reaches a child's heart.

Teachers, attuned to the chaos and violence of our times, are aware that schools have not escaped the modern mood of madness. What in the past was merely a classroom incident may now turn into a sit-in, a protest march, a demonstration, a strike.

The inner landscape of many children is full of mines ready to explode upon careless contact. Any insulting remark can set off an explosion.

SELF-DISCIPLINE

Discipline, like surgery, requires precision—no random cuts, no rambling comments. Above all, a teacher demonstrates self-discipline and good manners—no tantrums, no insults, no blistering language. The following common absurdity, described by an experienced teacher, must be avoided: "I have become aware of a personal paradox: I often use tactics similar to those that I try to eradicate in my pupils. I raise my voice to end noise. I use force to break up fighting. I am rude to a child who is impolite, and I berate a child who uses bad language."

A teacher never abdicates his moral authority. He does not enter mud-throwing contests with children. His discipline is never bizarre and his correction never sadistic. He lives by the law of compassion, even when challenged by children to defy it. A child often misbehaves in order to elicit reactions that confirm his negative views of adults. He provokes anger and evokes punishment to obtain proof for his convictions. He may be unaware of his

evocative powers and feel no responsibility for them.
Blindly he goes on creating incidents in which he
feels victimized. A teacher can help these children
best by refusing to dance to their tune, by declining
to follow their self-defeating designs. He does not
allow children to create his climate or to determine
his mood. They cannot constrict his repertory of
replies. He withholds predictable responses that
reinforce negative expectations. His words are
chosen, not triggered; his acts are selected, not
compelled.

In disciplining a child, a teacher must not be
motivated by personal pique ("I am going to see to
it personally, even if it's the last thing I do, that
you get what you deserve."). Private vendettas only
invite countervengeance. There is always danger in
punishment. It breeds brutality—sadistic or masochistic. While some children resent and take revenge
on their punitive teacher, others accept their role as
victims. Their masochistic needs compel them to
incite the teacher to degrade them, at least verbally.
Discipline is not a matter of fitting punishment to
crime and balancing books. It is the teacher's
generosity, not his accuracy, that counts. A teacher
is not a dictator. His formal powers are limited and
dwindling. His authority comes from competent
exercise of personal prestige and persuasion. His
best weapons are a cultured distaste for violence and
a civilized disbelief in punishment. For in the last

analysis, who is a true disciplinarian? He who can move children from terror to trust.

EMPHASIS ON PREVENTION

Misbehavior and punishment are not opposites that cancel each other; on the contrary, they breed and reinforce each other. Punishment does not deter misconduct. It merely makes the offender more cautious in committing his crime, more adroit in concealing his traces, more skillful in escaping detection. When a child is punished he resolves to be more careful, not more honest and responsible.

One high school student related, "Our teacher gave a long sermon on integrity. I listened and laughed inside. She herself teaches dishonesty and doesn't know it. I was late to school once because I overslept. She said, 'That's not a good excuse,' and she punished me. I got the message. The next time I was late, I made up a convincing story."

Punishment is pointless. It fails to achieve its goal. No child says to himself, while being punished, "I am going to improve. I am going to be a better person—more responsible, generous, and loving." Children know that punishment is rarely administered for their benefit, that it serves the needs of the punishing adult. The fact is, those who rely on retribution invite revenge. He who resorts to verbal vilification and physical force teaches violence. He who engenders hate becomes a partner in violence and an accessory to future crime.

How the blind belief in punishment is passed from generation to generation is dramatically illustrated in Willard Motley's book, *Knock on Any Door*. Upon hearing that his son Nick was sentenced to death for murder, his father said, "I can't understand it. . . . I always whipped him when he did wrong." Nick himself, in his death cell, has no better advice for the upbringing of his newborn nephew than "Don't let what happened to me happen to him. Beat the hell out of him. See that he does right."

Some parents and teachers ask, "Don't children have to be taught responsibility and respect, if not by persuasion, then by punishment?" Ethical concepts such as responsibility, respect, loyalty, honesty, charity, mercy cannot be taught directly. They can only be learned in concrete life situations from people one respects. One grows into virtue; one cannot be forced by punishment.

Few teachers believe in the efficacy of threats and punishment, yet they resort to them daily. Out of desperation they blame and shame, reproach and rebuke, threaten and punish. These methods not only fail to correct; they provide the troubled child with justification for past misbehavior and with an excuse for future offense.

Are there alternatives to punitive measures?
This chapter attempts to delineate alternatives.

NOTE PASSING

Through the corner of his eyes, the teacher saw Patricia passing a note to another girl. He jumped from his seat, pounced on Pat's friend and yanked the note out of her fingers. He started reading it aloud, but stopped suddenly. The note contained obscene adjectives attached to his name. The teacher's face reddened in rage.

"You dirty little so and so," he called out at Pat. "How dare you?"

Pat started crying.

"Your crocodile tears won't save you this time," said the teacher. "I want to see your parents and tell them what a disgusting daughter they brought up."

In this incident, the treatment was worse than the disease. The reaction of the teacher caused more damage than the passing of the note. The teacher made many mistakes. He turned a private indiscretion into a public disgrace. He escalated a misdemeanor into a felony. He lost his cool, used abusive language, and displayed rude manners.

Note passing has been a student's pastime since time immemorial. It may be disruptive, but it is not a crime. Procedures can be established to deal with it. Intercepted notes can be destroyed without being read by the teacher. This mail, though illegal, is not intended for his eyes. A teacher should not demonstrate unseemly conduct.

Children sometimes use notes to "put on" a naïve teacher. Knowing that the notes will be read, children contrive the content. In one class a young girl wrote three identical love letters, which were intercepted and read by three different teachers. Each of them asked her to stay after school to discuss the matter. But she went home leaving three teachers in search of *the* character.

"WHO PUT THE PEELS ON MY DESK?"

When the French teacher arrived in the classroom, he found a pile of orange peels on his desk. Face crimson, he turned to the children and growled, "Who put the peels on my desk?" There was no answer. "I will ask only once more who did it." There was silence. "He who did it," said the teacher loudly, "is not only a pig, he is a coward. I'll give you one more chance. Who did it?"

The teacher's eyes scanned the class to find the cowardly pig. No one volunteered. The teacher then assigned punishment to the whole class.

In this incident, the teacher committed many

mistakes. He demonstrated bad manners, displayed cruelty, and aroused hatred. Invectives do not invite confessions. Denunciations do not improve class morale. Collective punishment does not strengthen self-discipline.

This incident could have been handled effectively with a dash of humor. While putting the peels in the waste basket, the teacher could have commented: "To whom it may concern: I like peeled oranges, but not peels *sans* orange." Chances are that few children would have taken French leave from such a teacher.

A FOUR-LETTER WORD

Miss Armstrong, the fifth-grade teacher, overheard Oliver say a common four-letter word. Instead of ignoring it, she make a public issue of it.

TEACHER: What did you say?
OLIVER: What do you mean?
TEACHER: You know full well what I mean.
OLIVER: I said, "Oh, shoot."
TEACHER: That's not what you said.
OLIVER: That's exactly what I said.
TEACHER: That's not what I heard.
OLIVER: It's all in the ear of the beholder.

TEACHER: None of your smart-alecky talk. Leave the
  room!
OLIVER: The hell with this class.

Oliver ran out and closed the door with a bang.
The teacher stayed on to face a distraught class. In
this incident, the teacher unnecessarily escalated a
battle. It started with her asking a child to repeat
a dirty word and ended with her insulting him in
front of his friends. The whole fight could have
been avoided. A stern look would have been enough
to express disapproval. No talk was necessary.

THE POWER OF POETRY

It was snowing heavily. Several children
watched the snow through the half-frosted windows.
The teacher got angry. "What's the matter with
you? Haven't you ever seen snow? Anything is an
excuse for not paying attention. If you don't stop
looking out, I'll send you out into the cold. Last
warning! You understand?"

It is to be expected that children will want to
watch new snow. It is not in our interest to kill their
curiosity. Learning requires enthusiasm. The teacher
himself could have invited the children to celebrate
the occasion, to catch the magic of the moment, and

to watch the white wonder. Poetry would have won the day.

AFTER THE FALL

Howard, age ten, played a game called Anagrams. Some pieces fell on the floor and could not be found. The teacher said angrily, "You are very clumsy. You show no concern for class materials. You are not to play with this game again until you prove to me that you are capable of greater responsibility."

Howard reacted with anger. He sat sullenly for a while, then he started misbehaving. His pencil "fell off" the desk. His book "dropped" on the floor. He talked out of turn and had a fight with another child. His teacher related: "I knew I had handled the incident ineffectively and created a discipline problem. I regretted calling him names. Instead of attacking his personality attributes, I should have dealt with the event. Instead of preaching and threatening, I could have simply said: 'I expect you to take better care of class property.' I made a deliberate decision to act differently next time."

LACONIC LANGUAGE

Five-year-old Fred fought with a friend over a toy. The teacher pleaded with the boys to restore peace. The fight escalated. Instead of stopping the fight, the teacher made a speech: "I can see you will not be satisfied until you have injured each other. Each of you is determined to have his way. But I am as determined to have peace in this room. If you persist, I will have to do something drastic."

The boys ignored the teacher and continued their fight. The teacher got hold of the boys and gave another speech: "It's as hard for me to hold you as it is for you to be held. I know you don't like it. But I have reached a point now where I am doing what I feel I must." Bewildered, Fred looked at his teacher and said, "Then why don't you do something about it?"

The teacher should have stopped the fight without making a speech. A terse command in a tense voice was required. "No fighting and no hitting. It's against the values of this classroom. Use words, not fists."

Effective discipline requires that in moments of crisis teachers remain *laconic*. Strength is not conveyed by long explanations or arguing. Authority calls for brevity. To be firm is to be succinct.

LONG WORDS

Many teachers have learned to mobilize the English language to enforce discipline and maintain peace. Instead of threats and punishment, they use difficult words and a pocket dictionary. This approach helps them to keep cool and helps the child to enrich his vocabulary. The following example illustrates effective use of adult authority and English idiom.

When the teacher saw Leon, age six, punching his playmate, she said loudly, "I saw what happened. I am dismayed. I am aghast. I am chagrin . People are not for hurting." Leon was dumbfounded. He did not understand all the words, but he got the message.

The teacher used the incident to teach not only good behavior but also good English.

AVOIDING TRIVIA

A loud argument was heard in the class.

KAREN: Give me back my pencil.
LINDA: It's my pencil.
KAREN: You're a liar and a thief. You know it's mine.
LINDA: Shut your trap. You aren't getting my pencil
from me.

TEACHER (*with displeasure*): I heard both of you.
And I don't like what I heard. Let *me* have this
object of contention. Meantime, here is a
pencil for you and a pencil for you. Please decide after class whose pencil it is. And now,
back to work.

This was the end of the incident. It took the
teacher thirty seconds to settle it. The teacher intentionally avoided fruitless inquiries. He did not get
involved in a debate on the true ownership of this
private property. He prevented a pernicious pencil
from interfering with his lesson plans. With skill and
authority, he side-stepped time-consuming trivia: accusations, counter-accusations, contradictory testi-
monies, sentencing and policing.

"TO BE SORRY IS TO BEHAVE DIFFERENTLY"

Frank, age five, pinched his friend Sam. Sam
retaliated. A free-for-all followed. The teacher who
witnessed the incident said to Frank, "I saw it. People are not for pinching." Frank said, "I am sorry."
The teacher replied, "To be sorry is to make an
inner decision to behave differently." "O.K.,"

replied Frank. He went over to Sam to resume his play.

A VERBAL ATTACK

Victor, age ten, refused to stop talking in class. The teacher asked him, "Why do you find it necessary to talk out of turn?" "None of your business, mother f——" came his reply. Taken aback, the teacher answered, "What you just said makes me so angry that I feel I cannot talk to you." Victor was obviously surprised. He probably expected to be struck or berated. He remained silent throughout the rest of the period. When the class had left, Victor approached his teacher and stood near him in silence. Then he said, "You don't like me!" "Should I?" asked the teacher as he arranged papers on his desk. "Look, man, I'm sorry I called you that," cried out Victor. "If you're that sorry you'll demonstrate it in class," answered the teacher. Victor was taken aback by his teacher's response. He seemed to give it some thought.

ANGRY MOMENTS

Juan, age eight, a holdover in second grade, had alienated every teacher and every child he ever encountered. Aggressive and violent, · Juan over-reacted to the slightest provocation. He was often involved in fights and posed a serious threat to his class. During one such fight, his teacher said, "Juan, you seem angry. I can see by your face that you're very angry." "I sure am," he replied. "When you feel that angry, come to me and tell me about it." Juan was surprised at not being reprimanded. Now, periodically, he talks to his teacher about his anger, learning to translate physical aggression into symbolic speech. On another occasion Juan and Manuel were trying to organize a group of boys to play ball. Their frustration mounted and they began to fight. The teacher intervened and helped them set up the game. A while later, the two boys showed up, accusing each other of cheating. The teacher said: "It's such a pleasure to have two boys who can use words to tell exactly how they feel." Swelling with pride, the boys grinned at each other and settled their argument.

"I CAN SEE HOW ANGRY YOU ARE"

While washing the blackboards, Mario, age ten, managed to get a few drops of water on Jane. She grabbed the eraser, soaked it in water, and shoved it into his face. Mario went berserk He wanted to hurt her. The teacher held him back, saying, "You are so angry, it's not safe for Jane to be near you. Jane, please move to the other side of the class." Mario responded, "I'm going to beat the living daylights out of her." Teacher replied, "I can see how angry you are, and I can also hear your threats. Figure out another way to settle your grievances. We have too much violence as it is." Mario looked at his teacher with surprise. His anger subsided.

EXERCISES IN DISCIPLINE

While the class was doing independent reading, Carlo ran around the room annoying everyone in sight. "Carlo, it's hard to read while you're running," said the teacher. He stopped the running but began tearing paper and throwing it at other children. "People are not for annoying," the teacher said. Carlo did not respond. "Carlo, you need to make a decision, to stay with us or to leave," the teacher suggested. "I want to stay," Carlo responded.

A few minutes later Carlo was on the floor pinching other children. "I see you have made your decision, Carlo," the teacher said. "You've decided to leave the group." Carlo protested, but the teacher sat him down in the back of the room. When the period was over, Carlo came over and said, "I'm sorry, Teacher." "Your inner determination to do better is all the 'sorry' I need," answered the teacher. "I'll be better in the afternoon," promised Carlo.

He kept his word.

FIGHTING POLLUTION

Peter, age eight, gave his teachers a rough time. He often dropped books, spilled juice, and overturned chairs. He always managed to make a mess around him. Annoyed, his teacher insulted him directly: "How dare you make such a mess in the classroom. You are not fit to live in a pigsty." Peter listened but did not learn. He continued to create eyesores around him. Finally, he was assigned to another classroom.

The new teacher had a different approach. When he saw the mess, he said, "Peter, I am appalled at the sight of such a mess. It needs immediate cleaning." Peter cleaned up the mess. Pollution near his desk decreased noticeably. The teacher was effective because he said nothing about Peter. He did not criticize or call him names. Instead, he expressed his own feelings vividly and pointed out, factually, what needed to be done.

ENCOURAGING COOPERATION

Bert, age ten, specialized in interruptions. He lent his tongue to every conversation, uninvited. He shared his views on every subject, unasked. He meddled in foreign affairs and contributed irrelevancies to every interchange. His public proclamations taxed the patience of his teacher and his classmates. Bert ignored all rebukes and reprimands. He even interrupted the criticism about his interruptions. In desperation, the teacher wrote him the following note:

> Dear Bert,
> I am writing to enlist your cooperation. Please limit yourself to two verbal comments during each period. If you have something more to contribute, say it in writing. Use the enclosed notes and envelopes to mail me your comments. I am looking forward to your private correspondence.
>
> Sincerely,
> Your Teacher

Bert felt flattered to receive a letter from the teacher addressed to him. He read and reread it and made an effort to comply with the request.

A LETTER FROM THE TEACHER

Anthony, age seven, had been annoying his teacher. Leaning his chair back, he continually caused himself to fall and disturb the class. Talking to him had no effect. Finally, the teacher typed him a letter and *mailed* it to him. The note earnestly requested his cooperation in making the class a better place to work. It was very specific about the changes required.

The next day, Anthony came to school early. "You sent me a letter," he said. "Oh, you received it," the teacher said. "I never got a letter before," Anthony said. "I didn't know that my falling bothered everyone so much. I won't do it again." "Thank you, Anthony," said the teacher. As he was leaving, Anthony said, "Thank you for not telling my mother. She would have been mad."

Anthony didn't know that his mother called the teacher to thank her for the letter. She felt it was good for him to receive a grown-up letter addressed to him, about a matter concerning himself. "And thank you for leaving me out of it," his mother added.

TO SAVE A SOUL

The following story has a simple but universal moral: Kindness can only be taught kindly. Andy, age eight, was the scapegoat of his class. Children ganged up on him with insults and attacks. The chief bully and mischief-maker was Jay, age nine. When his teacher learned about this behavior, she became furious. Her first impulse was to punish him severely, "to give him a dose of his own medicine."

But she stopped herself. She explained, "I did not want to display more cruelty. He did not need an additional taste of the jungle. What he needed was a demonstration of civilization." To avoid arguments and to leave a more lasting impression, the teacher wrote Jay a note instead of arranging a face-to-face talk. The letter read:

Dear Jay,

Andy's mother has told me that her son has been made very unhappy this year. Name-calling and ostracizing have left him sad and lonely. I feel concerned about the situation. Your experience as a leader in your class makes you a likely person for me to turn to for advice. I value your ability to sympathize with those who suffer. Please

write me your suggestions about how we
can help Andy.

> Sincerely,
> Your Teacher

Jay never replied in writing, but his attacks on
Andy ceased.

Jay's teacher succeeded because she resisted the
temptation to berate and punish. She knew that the
niceties of life cannot be conveyed with a heavy
hand. Love can only be taught lovingly and compassion compassionately. Her appeal was intentionally couched in words that demonstrated concern.
It avoided criticism. It focused only on solutions.
The teacher talked to Jay's heart and pride, and he
responded helpfully.

"PUT IT IN WRITING"

A teacher in one of my seminars reported:
"For most of the year, the new ideas I introduced
in the classroom went virtually unnoticed by the
administration. The only mention came in a note
from the principal: 'Congratulations. You're the
only teacher who hasn't sent a child to the office this
month. You must be doing something right.'

"One day when I was in the main office, Walter ran in yelling, 'Quick, Russ is going to kill Carlos.' I followed Walter back to the classroom and the principal followed us. I saw the science teacher vainly yelling for quiet, while Carlos and Russ were rolling on the floor. I walked in, looked as angry as I could manage, and said with a voice full of indignation, *'I see two boys fighting on the classroom floor. We need words, not fist fights.'* The boys got up and Russ started yelling, 'He called my mother names.' Carlos interrupted, 'I did not. He called me a name.' *'I want the whole story in writing, from both of you,'* I said. 'But he . . .,' Carlos started. 'Put that on paper,' I said. 'I want to know in writing how it happened, how it developed; all the details. And your personal recommendations for the future.' The boys went to a corner of the room to write. I began to teach again, and the principal left. The whole incident took about five minutes. Later, the principal asked me for copies of the boys' papers. He mentioned the incident and read the papers at the next faculty conference. He suggested this method as a substitute for sending children to his office as punishment for fighting."

DEALING WITH COMPLAINTS

Paula, age nine, was a chronic complainer: "Teacher, Tim took my pencil." "Teacher, Jim is chewing gum." "Teacher, Ted is tearing up my papers." Her voice was disruptive, taxing the teacher's nerves. Finally he found a remedy. He told Paula: "Please submit all complaints in writing." It worked for a day. The next day she started voicing her complaints again. In a stern tone the teacher said: "To preserve the dignity of this class, all complaints must be submitted in writing." The problem subsided drastically.

One school adopted this rule as policy. Every classroom, including the kindergarten and first grade, had a complaint box. Though the young children could not yet write, they could draw. The children learned to express their grievances effectively. This method often prevents escalation of disciplinary problems. It saves time and energy and allows each teacher to deal with the complaints at her discretion.

A FACE-SAVING EXIT

"Whenever possible, avoid attributing a minor infraction to deliberate defiance. Allow for a face-saving exit." This maxim prevents many disciplinary problems. Example:

Barbara, age ten, broke a safety rule. She rode her bike in a playground full of children.

TEACHER: Barbara, an important safety rule in our school is, "No bike riding on the playground." It's too dangerous.

BARBARA: I forgot.

TEACHER: How can I help you remember?

BARBARA: I'll remember it from now on.

TEACHER: Your word is good enough for me.

Barbara left the yard grateful and relieved.

This minor infraction could have become a serious disciplinary problem had her teacher treated it so:

"Don't you know the rules?"

"Don't you have any consideration for other children?"

"For the rest of the week, leave your bike at home. Maybe this will teach you to obey the rules."

So often the fate of a conflict hinges on the teacher's response.

"INSIDE VOICES"

One day, as the noise in the classroom rose to unbearable levels, the teacher decided to let the children arrive at a set of rules for classroom decorum. At her prompting the children discussed the difference between "inside voices" and "outside voices" and the appropriate times for using them. The teacher found it more effective and more pleasant to say, "Shouldn't you be using your inside voices now, boys and girls?" than the dogmatic "Be quiet!"

IMPROVE OR TRANSFER

One public school has established several nongraded classes. Chronic disturbers of the peace are offered a choice: to improve or to transfer. No scolding, moralizing, or blaming is used. The child is told, "You can choose to keep the rules of this class or to transfer to another class. You decide."

The method has proved helpful. Moving to another class for a while gives both teacher and child a needed respite from each other. It cools tempers. A child may return to his regular class after his request is approved by his teacher.

THE CLASS AS A GROUP

A teacher can expect unpredictable group behavior in the classroom, and from the start he needs to deal with it effectively. Otherwise routine procedures may become persistent problems to plague the teacher and his class. Many emergencies can be forestalled if the teacher knows which methods are applicable to the prevention and resolution of group crises, and if he has techniques for implementing them.

What is it that teachers do that makes a difference in how children behave in the classroom? What methods create an effective "classroom ecology and learning milieu"? These questions were ingeniously researched by Jacob S. Kounin of Wayne State University and his associates. They video-taped real classes and studied the ongoing process. Some classes had a high rate of work involvement and a low rate of misbehavior. In other classes the rates were reversed. The question for the researchers was: "What do teachers do in the classroom that correlates with these different results?"

The researchers isolated specific categories of teacher style and behavior that correlated significantly with children's behavior in the classroom. These were:

"WITHITNESS"

An effective teacher demonstrates that he knows what is going on in the classroom. He does not pick on the wrong child for a deviant act of another. He singles out the initiator, not the onlooker, follower, or victim. He lives up to the proverbial picture of having "eyes in the back of his head."

"OVERLAPPING"

An effective teacher can attend to two issues simultaneously. While Mary was reading aloud, two boys in the seatwork area were talking. The teacher said. "Mary, continue reading. I'm listening," and almost instantly said to the boys, "I can hear you talk. Now turn around and do your seatwork."

This teacher took care of two issues without fuss and without loss of time and temper. In contrast, an ineffective teacher becomes immersed in a minor misbehavior, while dropping the main activity. Example:

Betty was reading aloud. Gary and Lee, in the seatwork region, were poking each other. The teacher

1. got up
2. put her reading book on her seat

3. walked over to the boys
4. stared at them and said angrily:
5. "I want this nonsense stopped!
6. "Right now!
7. "Lee, you haven't finished your arithmetic problems.
8. "Now get to them right now and get them right.
9. "And Gary, you too!"
10. She walked back to the reading circle.
11. She picked up her reading book.
12. She sat down on her chair and said
13. "All right. Now let's continue our story." *

In this incident, time, energy, and emotions were wasted needlessly.

"MOVEMENT MANAGEMENT"

In each classroom, children move physically (as from desk to reading circle) and psychologically (as from arithmetic to spelling). How teachers initiate, maintain, and terminate such moves significantly affects discipline in the classroom. Kounin's research shows that ineffective teachers overtalk and

* Jacob S. Kounin, *Discipline and Group Management in Classrooms*, p. 83. Numbers not in the original; added here for emphasis. See bibliography, page 319.

fail to maintain momentum in movements. Here is a list of their pitfalls:

1. *They "flip-flop"*: They terminate an activity, start another, and suddenly reverse themselves. Example: The teacher told the children to put away their spelling papers and take out their arithmetic books. They did. He then asked: "Who got all the spelling words right?"

2. *They "overdwell"*: They engage in a stream of talk and action much beyond what is required to achieve their goal. For example, see pages 113–115.

3. *They "fragment"*: They ask children to do singly what a whole group could be doing as a unit at one time. For an example, see pages 93–94.

4. *They are "stimulus-bound"*: Effective teachers are goal-directed; ineffective ones react to irrelevant minutiae and are easily deflected from their main activity. Example: In the middle of solving an arithmetic problem on the board, the teacher noticed a boy slouching in his seat. She stopped her work, left the board, walked over to his desk, and said: "Jimmy, sit up straight. How can you pay attention and write well when you're slouching like that? Now sit up real straight. . . . There, that's better." She then

walked back to the blackboard to resume her explanation.*

5. *They interrupt:* An effective teacher does not intrude on children's ongoing activities with sudden orders, questions, or statements. He is sensitive to the group's readiness to receive his message. An ineffective teacher bursts in on children, without waiting to be noticed. His own needs alone determine his timing and point of entry.

6. *They "dangle":* Ineffective teachers leave an activity dangling in midair and start another one. Example: A teacher was checking arithmetic seatwork. She called on Mary. Mary got up and was about to read, when the teacher looked around the room and said: "My now. Let's see. Suzanne isn't here, is she? Does anyone know why Suzanne is absent today?"**

GROUP FOCUS

Effective teachers focus on the group. During recitations they do not become immersed in one child. They have at their disposal a variety of techniques for alerting the class. Examples:

* Kounin, *Discipline and Group Management,* p. 99.
** Kounin, *Discipline and Group Management,* p. 101.

When selecting reciters in reading, Teacher A shows a flash card, asks who can read it, looks around the group *suspensefully*, then selects a reader. The whole group is alerted and involved. In contrast, Teacher B focuses immediately on one child ("John, will you read the card") and leaves the group in a passive role.

The difference between Teacher A and Teacher B relates to a multitude of classroom events. One deliberately creates suspense, alerts the class, and maintains group focus. The other behaves like a tutor to one child, not a teacher to a whole class. Kounin's study indicates that teachers who maintain group focus increase work involvement and reduce deviancy in their classes.

A Personal Note

I have emphasized Kounin's studies for two reasons. One, they focus on prevention rather than on handling of misbehavior. Two, his techniques for creating an effective "classroom ecology and learning milieu" are devoid of punitiveness. The stress of these studies is on concreteness and description, not on slogans and clichés. Every teacher knows that "love is not enough." Neither is "creating rapport" or "making it interesting." Friendly adjectives do not classroom problems solve: A teacher can be "warm," "patient," and "loving" and still be unable to survive in a classroom.

Teaching demands not just desirable personality attributes but specific skills. To paraphrase Kounin: Skills are not ends in themselves but they are necessary tools. Techniques are enabling; their absence acts as a barrier. The focus on skills is not opposed to a concern for individual children; rather it enables the teacher to plan for individual differences.

TO SIDE WITH THE HIDDEN ASSET

It is said that nature always sides with the hidden flaw. Teachers have the opposite role: to side with the hidden asset, to minimize a child's deficiencies, intensify his experience, and enlarge his life. In every classroom encounter a teacher asks himself: "How can I be helpful right now?" This approach avoids finding faults, establishing guilt, and meting out punishment. Teachers become experts in prevention of dissension, virtuosi in avoidance of crises, masters in de-escalation of conflict. Disciplinary problems become opportunities for conveying values, providing insights, and strengthening self-esteem.

CHAPTER 7

When Child and Teacher Clash: The Parent's Role

A Blueprint for Help. An Angry Letter.

It Takes a Mother and a Father.

Redirecting Anger. A Dose of Trust.

Sympathetic Acknowledgment.

"Save It for Home." Restoring Self-Esteem.

"I Wish He Didn't Talk Like That."

Becoming Mature. The Rejected Project.

A Second Chance. A Poor Report Card.

Scientific Curiosity. A Focused Interview.

To Change an Attitude. To Mirror a Wish.

A Letter to a Principal.

Two Letters to a Teacher.

"I Hate Her! I Hate Her! I Hate Her!"

Solution-Oriented. Lessons That Linger.

When a teacher and a child clash, what is a parent to do? Should he take the teacher's side and reinforce his authority, or should he support his own child against the harsh world? Or is there another alternative? The following episodes describe methods of intervention which avoid taking sides. They focus on solving problems and strengthening self-esteem.

A BLUEPRINT FOR HELP

Earl, age ten, came out of his room, tense and agitated: "I can't finish my homework," he called. "My teacher gave me a crazy punishment. I have to write fifty times, 'If I stop fooling around, I will be able to learn something.' I wrote it ten times already. I can't do any more. What are you going to do about it, Mom?"

Mother (*taken aback*): "I need some time to think, Earl."

Earl went back to his room, choking back tears. Mother stood in shocked silence, carrying on an internal monologue: "My son feels so defeated about school. For him, writing is torture. This punishment will only embitter him more. How can I help him right now?" Mother made the following mental notes:

Show concern, but don't attack the teacher.

Convey this message: We cannot change the teacher, but we can endure the situation.

Allow expression of negative feelings. Acknowledge them and offer token help.

Mother went into her son's room, fortified by her blueprint. She found Earl in bed, sullen and teary.

MOTHER: Did the teacher really tell you to copy this sentence fifty times?

EARL: She sure did. Do you know what she does with the paper when you bring it? She just rips it up—in front of everybody—and throws it in the wastebasket.

MOTHER: Oh, no. Are you being serious? I can see why you're outraged.

EARL: I'll get out of her class. I'll be real bad, so she'll transfer me to a lower grade. Since I can't be the smartest, I'll be the dumbest. I won't do any work, and I won't understand anything.

MOTHER: You're even thinking of doing poor work, just to get rid of her. You must feel very hurt and bitter.

EARL: I do. I do.

MOTHER: Earl, I agree with you. Copying doesn't make children behave better. It just hurts their dignity.

EARL: What's dignity?

MOTHER: The respect we feel for ourselves.

EARL: But I still have to write that stupid thing another forty times.

MOTHER: And that won't be easy. It may take an hour or even longer. I'd like to help you. It's such a tough assignment. Where shall I focus the light—on the bed or the desk?

EARL: On my bed.

MOTHER: Think you'll be more comfortable there? (*She focuses the light, props him up with pillows and gets him a hard book to put the paper on.*) Earl, would you like some raisins to nibble on while you work?

EARL: Yes, please.

Nibbling raisins, Earl started working on his assignment. Every few minutes he came over to show his mother his production and to be applauded for his efforts.

EARL: Well, I did it all!

MOTHER: You made up your mind to do the job and you stuck to it. I admire your perseverance.

EARL: Now she can rip it to pieces.

(*He purses his lips, frowns, scrutinizes both sides of the paper, pretends to count, and then slowly rips an imaginary sheet.*)

MOTHER: You wish she wouldn't rip it.

EARL (*smiles wryly*): Yeah! That'll be the day. Well, good night, Mother.

Off he went to bed.

AN ANGRY LETTER

Jean, age thirteen, came home angry at the teacher. She complained about his curt manners and rough language. She wanted to be transferred to another class. Mother asked her to put her grievance in writing. Jean handed her mother a self-explanatory letter addressed to the teacher:

To my teacher, the tyrant:

I'd like you to know that you are one of the main reasons I'm leaving this class. I pity any child taught by you. I wish you had a teacher like yourself. You would deserve each other. You are selfish, inconsiderate, and full of unearned pride. You never say anything nice to me. You are always mean and rough. "Shut up, be quiet, stupid": That's all you know.

You can't do anything to me because, fortunately, I am out of your power. If I weren't, I'd be dead.

You are the only person (if it's legal to call you that) I've ever hated.

> With malice in my heart,
> A Former Student

Mother read the letter aloud, slowly and deliberately. Jean listened attentively. The letter truly expressed her feelings. She was delighted to hear her words in her mother's voice. Her anger diminished. The letter was never mailed.

IT TAKES A MOTHER AND A FATHER

SANDY (*age fourteen*): I hate the typing teacher. Maybe I am stupid, but I cannot learn from her. How come I'm so dumb in typing?

MOTHER: Dumb? I don't approve of your insulting my daughter.

SANDY: You should hear how this teacher insults us.

She only likes the quick kids. She can't stand the rest of us. She hasn't even memorized our names. Imagine, insulting people whose names she can't remember.

MOTHER: I see you're having a rough time in typing class.

SANDY: How can I learn from someone I don't respect?

MOTHER: Even if you want to learn, something in you revolts against it.

SANDY: That's right. That's exactly right. I'm supposed to practice at home, but I am not going to. I just don't care any more. (*Father, who has overheard the conversation between mother and daughter, comes in from the living room.*)

FATHER: I need help in typing my résumé. I have put it off too long. I need it for tomorrow.

SANDY: Would you want me to type it, Dad? Would you trust me with your résumé?

FATHER: It would really be a big help to me.

SANDY: How many copies do you need?

FATHER: Two.

SANDY: I'll do an extra one, in case you need one in the future. (*Sandy races down the stairs, sets up the typewriter, types the résumé, and brings it to her father.*)

FATHER: Thank you, Sandy. You've really helped me out. And at such short notice.

SANDY: You're welcome. Come to think of it, I'm the only one in this family who uses the touch system. I hardly looked at the keys at all. Anytime you need a typist, just whistle.

Sandy's mother added the following comments: "This episode could have easily ended in a debacle, had I given my daughter the usual critical 'advice': 'You always exaggerate. Your teacher isn't that bad. If you aren't the teacher's pet, you get jealous and bitter. Don't you realize how lucky you are to have the opportunity to learn typing? You'll need it in high school and college—some teachers insist on typed reports. So don't cut off your nose to spite your face.' "

REDIRECTING ANGER

Eddie came home for lunch in a morose mood. He growled at his mother and fought with his sister.

MOTHER: I cannot permit you to upset the household. Apparently, you are upset. Tell your anger in words. (*Eddie throws himself on the couch and starts to sob.*)

EDDIE: We had a substitute teacher this morning.

What a meany. She gave me extra homework
for tonight. I hate her! I don't want to go back
to school today.

MOTHER: I can see that you are very upset by her.
It must have been difficult for you to control
yourself in class.

EDDIE: Yeah, I felt like getting up and hitting her.

MOTHER: And you still have to face her all afternoon. That takes courage and inner strength.

EDDIE: Yeah. I hope I can stand it. I said plenty of
things under my breath about her.

MOTHER: You can hardly wait for your regular
teacher to come back.

EDDIE: I sure can't.

MOTHER: I'll bet there is much more you can tell me
about how angry you feel. Here's a pencil and
paper. Put your anger in writing. You know,
that's what *creativity* is.

EDDIE: I don't have time to be creative now. I have
to go back to school. I don't want to be late.
(*He puts on his coat and returns to school.*)

A DOSE OF TRUST

Scene: *Breakfast*
BETH (*age ten*): I don't want to go to school. I hate
it.

MOTHER (*with sympathy*): I know. It's not easy for you this year. You have a strict teacher. I even know that he yells a lot and you don't like it at all.

BETH: You can say that again. He is the roughest teacher I ever had.

MOTHER: I know.

BETH: You can't make me go to school. When you drop me off, I could play hooky.

MOTHER: You could, but I believe you wouldn't.

BETH: How do you know?

MOTHER: I trust you. (*Beth relaxes. No amount of logic could have accomplished what a dose of trust did.*)

SYMPATHETIC ACKNOWLEDGMENT

Barry, age eleven, came home tense and dejected. "Did something happen at school?" his mother asked. "Yes," said Barry angrily. "The teacher pulled my hair and it hurt. Two boys and I were fooling around in the hall. We were too noisy. He could have said, 'Boys, no more of that' or 'Not here' or 'No fooling.' Instead he attacked me."

Mother answered, "You wish he used more civilized ways? I agree."

Barry seemed relieved.

"SAVE IT FOR HOME"

The teacher called to complain about ten-year-old Warren. "He has been acting very silly, disrupting the entire class," she told his mother. "I make the children laugh," Warren admitted. "I do funny things, like a comedian." Mother said, "I'll bet it must be very tempting to make the whole class laugh, but your teacher is very angry at you." Warren said, "I think I better stop." Mother said, "It won't be easy to control yourself. You'll be tempted to crack a joke. When you feel like saying something funny, save it for home. We can laugh about it together." Warren liked the idea. His behavior in class improved.

Mother was brief and helpful. She did not question, threaten, or punish. She reported the teacher's displeasure to her son, expressed appreciation for his willingness to improve, and suggested an acceptable outlet for his funny impulse.

RESTORING SELF-ESTEEM

Tim, age nine, returned from school upset. His English teacher called him "irresponsible and unreliable." "Since you dawdle in the bathroom," she told him, "you won't go there alone any more. Someone will accompany you."

Tim was indignant and insulted. He recalled other insults and injuries by this teacher. "Once, I told her I found gum in the schoolyard, and she replied, 'You are a known liar, Tim.' And once when I graded myself high on an honesty chart she made fun of me. She said, 'You? Honest? Don't make me laugh.' "

Mother listened to his tales of terror and her anger rose. "That teacher is playing havoc with my son's self-image," she thought. Tim continued to spit out his poison. Mother shook her head in sympathy. Then she said, "Son! Your teacher has the wrong boy. I'd like to tell her how responsible you are. Doesn't she know that when you find money you return it? I'd like to tell her that it's you I put in charge of the downstairs doors when Daddy and I are not home."

Tim interrupted: "Tell her how you gave me the pruning shears to cut the forsythia bushes when you couldn't even trust the gardener." "Yes," said Mother, "and how about the can of poison spray I gave you to kill dandelions—because I knew that it was in good hands."

"Yes," agreed Tim, "and tell her I hate her!" Tim was still upset. Mother said, "Do you think a note describing your feelings of anger would help?" "It can't hurt," he answered.

On a sheet of paper, Tim elaborated in detail his feelings of anger and his fantasies of revenge. Then he tore up the paper into tiny shreds and felt less upset.

"I WISH HE DIDN'T TALK LIKE THAT"

A teacher was drilling a hole in the wall. The bit got stuck. Randy, age twelve, said, "May I make a suggestion? How about putting the bit in the drill and backing it out." The teacher replied, "You know what your suggestion is worth? Exactly what you charged me: nothing!" Randy looked at his teacher in sheer hatred and left the room.

When Randy told his story to his father, he got angry: "Why do you always have to make suggestions? The teacher did not ask for your advice. Why do you have to open your mouth? Why don't you mind your own business?"

Randy became hysterical. "You are worse than the teacher," he shouted. "He is a stranger, you are my father. You know nothing, and you understand nothing." And he ran out of the house.

When a child is angry, he needs an attentive ear, not a slashing tongue. He needs an adult to diminish his rage, not to increase his fury. Randy had made a civil suggestion, which his teacher rejected rudely. Father could have said, "You made such a sensible suggestion, and you were met with such a rude response. That hurts. I wonder what bugged your teacher? I wish he didn't talk to you like that." Randy would have loved his father for his support at that moment.

BECOMING MATURE

KARL (*age ten*): I got sent to the office today.

MOTHER: Tell me about it.

KARL: When I came back from lunch, I took my seat, only the chair was turned around, so I sort of straddled it.

MOTHER: That made the teacher angry?

KARL: Well, yeah. Then she said, "Karl, turn your seat around this minute." So I did. I turned my whole seat around and sat in the same position —only this time I was facing the class.

MOTHER: And that made everybody laugh.

KARL (*laughing*): Yeah. And then she sent me to the office.

MOTHER (*sighing*): Now I understand why Dad has been called to school for a conference about you. (*There is a minute of silence.*)

KARL: Gee, Mom, I'm sorry. It won't happen again.

MOTHER: I've noticed that when you aim for something you achieve it.

KARL (*the next day*): The teacher asked for a sentence with the verb "hide." I was tempted to yell, "Dirt can't hide with intensified Tide," and crack up the class. But I restrained myself. How about that?

MOTHER: You have become your own boss. You have learned to decide when to say something and when not to say something. I like this quality of yours. That's what I call becoming a mature individual.

THE REJECTED PROJECT

Kenny, age eleven, came home from school angry. His Social Studies project had been rejected. "The teacher said it's sloppy," he complained. "I spent so much time on the project. Now I don't know what to do."

Mother answered, "I saw you working hard and I know you are disappointed." "I don't feel like doing anything for this teacher," Kenny said. "She did manage to discourage you," replied Mother. "This I regret." "Maybe I'll give it another try," ventured Kenny. He went into his room to tackle his assignment.

In this incident, his mother was most helpful. She did not blame her son or the teacher for the rejection of the assignment. She did not say, "Why didn't you do a better job? You are in the fifth grade now. You are not a little child any longer. If you played less and worked more, you wouldn't be in trouble." Instead, Mother acknowledged his predicament with tact and compassion. Her emotional supports enabled Kenny to tackle the task.

A SECOND CHANCE

Bill, age twelve, and his friend Michael had been very disruptive in class. Michael was demoted. Bill was shocked.

BILL (*to his mother*): I can't take it any more! The teacher wants to break me and get rid of me like she did Michael.

MOTHER: Tell me about it.

BILL: Every morning she tells me, "I don't want to hear anything from you today." I never had a teacher who refused to call on me. She doesn't trust me. She doesn't accept improvement. I asked her why she was doing this to me. She gave me a mean look and walked out of the room. I have the feeling that she'll never change. I don't have a chance. Even an ex-convict is given a second chance.

MOTHER: How exasperating that situation must be for you. I'll give this matter my full attention. I need time to think about a solution. It's a difficult problem.

BILL: That's putting it mildly.

MOTHER: You could put it more strongly, in writing, if you want to.

Bill wrote the following poem:

Mrs. T. is so mean to me,
She makes me wish she were stuck in a tree.
How would I feel if she disappeared?
If this great miracle came to be
I'd feel good, and happy and free!

MOTHER: You certainly expressed your feelings strongly. Be assured that Daddy and I will give this matter our full consideration.

Mother's words and his poem reduced Bill's anger and diminished his tension. When Father came home, Bill presented him his problem. Together they decided on a course of action: Father would see the teacher to discuss resumption of friendly relations between her and Bill.

A POOR REPORT CARD

Mary, age thirteen, received a poor report card. It included a C in science. Mary complained, "It should have been a B, but the teacher doesn't like me. He gives marks based on his feelings toward a student."

"You really feel you deserve a B," answered her mother. "I sure do," said Mary. "Would you like me to talk to your teacher and bring it to his attention?" asked Mother.

"No," said Mary, "I'll get through the year on my own."

Mother avoided futile arguments and needless scenes. She did not ask provocative questions: "How come the teacher picks on you? You must have done something to irritate him. What did you do?"

When Mother was sympathetic and helpful Mary could assume responsibility for her own life.

SCIENTIFIC CURIOSITY

Lester, age eight, irritated his teachers with his scientific questions. He complained to his mother about their impatience. "There are so many things I want to know. For instance, if the earth stopped spinning would the people fall off? Would they disintegrate? If the moon were ten million miles from the sun would it freeze? My teacher says, 'Stop asking foolish questions. Curiosity killed the cat.' I told her I am curious, but I am not a cat. She got angry at me and told me to shut up."

Mother responded: "I can see you're bursting with scientific curiosity. You ask important questions. They need to be written down. Here is paper and a pencil. Ask in writing." Lester wrote down his questions, then rewrote them neatly. Mother included his list in a note sent to the teacher, requesting her help.

Mother intentionally abstained from futile explanations ("Teachers have no time for such questions. What would happen if everyone in the class did that? You are too curious for your own good. Do your work! That's all that is required of you."). Instead of criticism, Mother offered appreciation. She supported curiosity and diverted it into the right channels.

A FOCUSED INTERVIEW

Lynn was an honor student in all subjects. But her grades in algebra were low. She once asked her teacher to explain the relevance of algebra to life. He replied, "Don't analyze, memorize!" He became angry when he heard that Lynn was rehearsing for a school play, singing in the chorus, and playing the piano. "You are busy with everything but math," he accused her, and invited her mother for a conference.

TEACHER (*with sarcasm*): I guess Lynn knew you were coming in for a conference. She suddenly started to participate in class.

MOTHER (*avoiding a trap*): Obviously, Lynn needs extra help in algebra. Would you suggest a tutor?

TEACHER: Don't waste your money on a tutor. Lynn can come to me for help. I am not always available. She can check with me, if she's interested.

MOTHER: Since you do have such a heavy responsibility at school, I would appreciate your recommendation for a tutor. That would be most helpful for Lynn.

TEACHER: O.K. If that's what you want. Learning algebra is cumulative. She may have to start at the beginning.

MOTHER: I trust you and the tutor to decide the best method of reviewing the material.

A tutor was found, a college girl, whom Lynn liked. "She makes math reasonable and relevant," Lynn commented. "She ties things together and makes sense. She understands the subject and really wants to help me."

In this episode Mother avoided arguments. She did not take the teacher's bait and managed to side-step his provocations. She focused on finding solutions and helping her daughter.

TO CHANGE AN ATTITUDE

ELLEN: I absolutely deplore the study of mythology. It's not relevant to my present life. I just hate it. It's boring and foolish. In fact, I plan to challenge my English teacher. I want to know why we need to learn Greek, Roman, and Norse mythology.

MOTHER: I see you have strong feelings about mythology.

ELLEN: I suppose you think that some day I will see the connection between fairy tales and reality.

MOTHER: Yes. But you are entitled to your negative feelings about mythology.

Scene: *Three days later . . .*

ELLEN: What a fascinating subject it can be—really, beautiful.

MOTHER: Which subject, dear?

ELLEN: Mythology. Miss Brady really makes it exciting. *Good teachers can really light the way for their students.* I've analyzed its relevance to our present life and times. It's so psychological. Each character represents our various emotions and human relationships.

Flushed and bubbling, Ellen went on telling Mother all she had learned about the timelessness of myths.

A glance at this page will reveal why Mother was helpful. She talked so little. She explained nothing. She did not defend Greek mythology and did not offend her daughter's psychology. She accepted, without judging, Ellen's present feelings, confident in her daughter's ability to learn and to change.

TO MIRROR A WISH

Mel, age twelve, complained to his mother about his Social Studies teacher.

MEL: She doesn't grade papers, doesn't check homework, and doesn't have interesting class discussions. She is just an old, senile grump.

MOTHER: You are unhappy with your teacher.

MEL: Mom, she is so dull.
MOTHER: You wish you had an exciting teacher.
MEL: I wish I had Mr. R. He is great.
MOTHER: You wish you were in his class.
MEL: I do. Anyplace but in Mrs. S.'s class.
MOTHER: I know.

The incident ended quickly and quietly. Mother was helpful because she attended to her son's feelings and wishes. She did not defend the teacher or explain the situation. She avoided mouthing platitudes ("You can learn from anyone if you really want to."). Mel left the conversation feeling understood. That is what children most often want from their parents.

A LETTER TO A PRINCIPAL

Amy, age eight, was assigned to a teacher reputed to be stern, cold, and loud. Amy's father sent a letter to the principal:

Dear Dr. C.:
In my effort not to be an "interfering parent," I ignored an impulse to call you for an appointment last spring. However,

my concern for my daughter's emotional and academic development demands that I communicate with you at this time.

The placement card received in the mail today indicates that Amy has been assigned to Mrs. J.'s class. Word of mouth makes me suspect that this would be a mistake for my child.

In her first two years of school, Amy's teachers created environments for her that made her flourish. In the last year, I saw this growth inhibited by teachers who were impatient, emotionally inaccessible, and out of tune with everyday human needs of an individual child. I would be remiss in my parental responsibility if I did not request a transfer to another teacher.

We appreciate your past cooperation and know that the needs of children are uppermost to you.

I am looking forward to hearing from you.

The letter had an impact. The principal called the teacher's attention to her reputation among parents. The teacher made an effort to improve her behavior and image.

TWO LETTERS TO A TEACHER

The following letter was written by an eight-year-old girl to her school music teacher:

Dear Teacher,
My name is Rose. I am in your music class. I think it is not fair that you always pick Hilda for all the special solos. Other children need a chance, too. Sometimes you can choose me. I don't mean to brag, but I'm always on pitch, and I have a good ear and a good voice. May I have at least O-N-E special solo?

Sincerely yours,
Rose

The teacher did not acknowledge the receipt of her letter. He considered it "cute" and showed it to the principal, but the complaint was ignored. A month later Rose's father sent a letter to the teacher (with a copy to the principal).

Dear Mr. M.:
Some time ago my daughter wrote a letter to you describing a situation which was bothering her. To my knowledge, you

have not responded in any way. We have taught our children to express their complaints with dignity and respect.

Even a noncommittal reply such as "I have received your letter and am studying it" would have indicated to her that "going through channels" can be effective. But no response? Is that what students mean when they complain of lack of communication with the Establishment? As my daughter said, "You see, Daddy. It was only a waste of time."

I would appreciate your comments on this matter.

Rose's father related: "Shortly thereafter, Mr. M. responded: He gave Rose a solo in the spring concert. Sad to say, though, he missed the real point of the issue."

"I HATE HER! I HATE HER! I HATE HER!"

Paul, age sixteen, and six feet tall, lived through a harassing experience. It could have ended in disaster but for his mother's competent intervention.

When Paul handed his English composition to the teacher, she gave it a cursory look and said, "It's not good enough to grade." She crumpled the paper and threw it into the wastebasket. Paul's mind went blank. Enraged, he started moving toward the teacher but then veered toward the door and ran out of the class. He ran all the way home—three miles. He threw his book on the floor, shouting.

PAUL: I hate her! I hate her! I hate her!

MOTHER: Whatever happened, it must have really gotten at your guts.

PAUL: This damn teacher, she didn't even read the paper. She just balled it up and threw it in the garbage.

MOTHER: How humiliating!

PAUL: It was murder.

MOTHER: I bet you felt like striking her.

PAUL (*in sheer surprise*): Mom! Mom! What did you say?

MOTHER: I said you must have felt violent.

PAUL: Yes! Yes! Yes!

His anger subsided. He picked up his books from the floor and went upstairs. When he came down, he was calm enough to return to school.

SOLUTION-ORIENTED

Mary, age ten, had been chosen to play first violin in her school orchestra. On the way to a concert, she stumbled over a curb; the case fell out of her hands, and the violin cracked. Mary was too wretched even to cry. "I'm so clumsy," she wailed. "Now I won't be able to play the concert and it's all my fault."

"That's not what we say when a mishap occurs," said Mary's mother. "We don't blame. We are solution-oriented. The question is: How can we get another violin tonight?" Mary's mouth dropped open. "Mrs. Lee, the music teacher, has extras in the music room," she said meekly. "You just found the solution!" said Mother with appreciation.

Mary and her mother hurried to the music room. Mary told Mrs. Lee what had happened. Mrs. Lee started yelling, "You broke your instrument? When we give you a violin, we expect you to take care of it. You'll have to pay for it. Violins are expensive. I don't know if I should give you another one."

"Mrs. Lee," said Mary loudly, "we need to be solution-oriented. I'll pay for the damage tomorrow. Right now, I need a violin for the concert."

Mrs. Lee seemed dumbstruck. She handed a

violin to Mary, who rushed backstage to tune it for the concert.

Mary's mother performed a great service to her daughter. She taught her a most important principle in mental health: When things go wrong, a responsible person does not look for culprits. He looks for solutions.

LESSONS THAT LINGER

As this chapter illustrates, schools fail when they stifle the spirit, muddle the mind, and oppress the heart. Yet given the skills, teachers, like the parents in the vignettes, can communicate to a child without enraging him. They can change their destructive responses and acquire new ways of offering criticism, venting anger, dealing with discipline, and inviting cooperation. While there is no master key that opens all doors of communication, there are keys that open doors.

Thomas Mann said: "Speech is civilization itself." Yet words can brutalize as well as civilize, injure as well as heal. Teachers, like parents, need a language of compassion, a language that lingers lovingly. They need words that convey feelings, responses that change moods, statements that tempt good will, answers that bring insight, replies that radiate respect. The world talks to the mind. A teacher speaks more intimately; he talks to the heart. And the heart is nourished by subtleties—by a glance that appeals, a nod that affirms, and a comment that confirms. Education translates experience into values. To reach the eternal in value, it must touch helpfully on the immediate in experience.

CHAPTER 8

Homework

An Effective Approach.
Respect for Autonomy. An Appeal to Pride.
"Homework Is Between You and Your
Teacher." By Candlelight. "I Hate School."
Lost Assignments. Father's Turn.
Emotional Support. Anger and English.
The Power of Acknowledgment.
Poor Grades. "A Challenging Assignment."
New Words. A Note of Truth.
Mother Learns. A Mood of Mutuality.
The Right Help. Aid: A Child's View.
"A Personal Responsibility."

AN EFFECTIVE APPROACH

Teachers devote much time to assigning and checking homework. Many classroom comedies and tragedies revolve around it. Children learn to lie about homework, copy it from friends, "lose" it on the way to school, or "forget" it at home.

One school established effective procedures of dealing with homework. A child who fails to do or bring his homework must write a formal note stating what was not done and when it will be in. No "why" questions are asked. It is taken for granted he had his reasons. He is not forced to make up believable excuses and convincing lies. The letter is put on file. When the homework is made up, the letter is returned to the child. Thus, each pupil is responsible for his own ledger: evidence of diligence or deficiency is in his own handwriting. The child is given the motivation and opportunity to improve his record.

Parents often do not know how to help their

children with homework. When they get a negative note from a teacher, they get angry, yell, nag, and punish. Parents need guidance in how to help their children cope with assignments. The following vignettes describe helpful ways of dealing with homework.

RESPECT FOR AUTONOMY

Life is easier when parents deliberately ignore the daily details of their child's homework. School assignments are the responsibility of the child and his teachers. As one father said to his son, "Homework is for you what work is for me—a personal responsibility." When parents become passionately involved with homework and grades, a child may rebel and sink to the bottom of his class. If nagging and checking interfere with this autonomy, failing may become a symbol of independence. As one child said, "My parents can take away my allowance and TV set, but they can't take away my failing grades."

A child cannot grow up if he functions as an extension of his mother. To mature, he needs to sense his separateness and individuality, and to know that he is a person with a mind of his own. Even when adults make demands, they can support his autonomy by allowing him a voice and a choice in matters that affect his life.

Bruce, age eight, habitually procrastinated doing his homework. Arguments and spoiled moods were daily affairs. "Bruce, did you do your homework? Why do you always have to postpone and delay? Do you want to fail school? You are so lazy. All you do is watch TV." One day his mother changed her approach. Instead of threats, she offered him a choice. She said, "Bruce, you can do your homework right after school or after dinner, before television. You decide." Bruce chose to do his homework after dinner.

AN APPEAL TO PRIDE

A letter of complaint arrived from school. Ivan, age ten, was behind in his studies. His father's first reaction was to call his son and give him a verbal thrashing: "Listen, son, from now on you are going to do your homework every day, including weekends and holidays. No movies. No TV and no more visits to friends. We have never had illiterates in our family, and you are not going to be the first. I am personally going to make sure that you get down to business."

This speech had been delivered many times be

fore. It always resulted in an angry atmosphere, a furious father, and a defiant son. The increased pressure only increased Ivan's resistance. He became an expert in evasion and concealment.

This time, Father avoided threats and punishment. Instead, he appealed to his son's pride. In a private conference, he showed Ivan his teacher's letter and said, "Son, we do expect scholarship from you. The world needs capable people. There are still so many problems that need solutions." Ivan was so taken by his father's words and tone of voice that he said, "I promise to take my work more seriously."

"HOMEWORK IS BETWEEN YOU AND YOUR TEACHER"

Jeff, age twelve, unsuccessfully tried to involve his mother in doing his homework. Mother refused, saying, "Homework is your responsibility." His sister, Betsy, age eight, liked to do homework. However, one afternoon when she was forbidden to visit a friend, she threatened defiantly, "If you don't let me go, I won't do my homework." Before Mother had a chance to respond, Jeff said, matter-of-factly, "Homework is between you and your teacher."

BY CANDLELIGHT

Rachel, age nine, started doing her homework when the lights went out. It was a general blackout. "What am I going to do?" she asked her mother. "How will I finish my assignments?" Mother invited Rachel into the kitchen and lit some candles. By candlelight, Mother did her cooking, and Rachel her homework. When Rachel finished, Mother said, "You finished in spite of the darkness. It certainly took determination and perseverance. It is not easy to do complex assignments by the light of a candle." Rachel seemed to grow before Mother's eyes. Later in the evening, Mother told Father how Rachel executed her work all on her own, in spite of the blackout. Rachel, attentive and joyous, put the finishing touch to the story. She said, "Sure, I am a responsible kid."

"I HATE SCHOOL"

Bob burst into the house screaming, "I hate school. They give too much homework. I want to quit." His mother suggested that he spend about one hour each day on homework. Bob became angrier. He screamed, "I am quitting, and that's that." Mother yelled back in anger, "I don't care if you do the homework or not. You are going to school." Bob kept on crying hysterically. "I am not doing any more homework. I am quitting."

Then the light dawned on Bob's mother. She said, "Son, I hear you. You are telling me that you really hate that place." His eyes brightened and he said, "Yes-s-s-s." "I'll bet you wish that the building would crumble to the ground brick by brick," Mother ventured. "Yes," came a quick reply. As if by magic, his anger subsided. He went into his room and did his homework.

LOST ASSIGNMENTS

In the following episode, a mother solved a persistent problem by turning away from ineffective punishment to effective communication.

Dwight, age nine, wrote his school assignments on pieces of paper, which he habitually managed to misplace. He spent many hours looking for the "lost" materials. In anger, Mother raved and ranted, threatened and punished, attacked and insulted. But Dwight continued his defeating practice. Dwight's mother decided to change her approach. When she and Dwight were in an especially comfortable mood, she approached him:

MOTHER: Dwight, I see you are still not using the assignment book. I wish you would. I wish you had more time for play, instead of looking for lost little pieces of paper.

DWIGHT: I promise I will use my assignment book starting tomorrow.

MOTHER: That's good enough for me.

DWIGHT: What do you mean?

MOTHER: If you say you'll use it, I know you will, because you are a man of your word.

Dwight scribbled a few words in his notebook and said, "I wrote myself a reminder."

FATHER'S TURN

In the following episode, a mother avoided trouble by allowing Father to deal with the situation. She knew that she was too upset to tackle it herself.

Mother was angry at herself because she had allowed ten-year-old Ethel to watch TV before doing homework. Bedtime arrived and homework had not been done. Mother asked Father to talk to her.

FATHER: Time for bed!
ETHEL (*angrily*): I have to finish my homework!

With this reply, she began twisting all over her chair, until she fell on the floor. Ethel looked up at her father, waiting for a rebuke. Instead, he held out his hand to her and said, "Hope you didn't hurt yourself, honey." As he helped her up she threw her arms around him in gratitude and love.

FATHER: You can have ten more minutes to finish your homework. Then it will be time to get ready for bed.
ETHEL: I'll get ready for bed first and then take ten, okay?
FATHER: If you want to.

She readied herself in record time, came into the kitchen, gave Father another hug and went to finish her homework. Ten minutes later she was in bed, smiling and satisfied.

Ethel's mother helped her daughter and herself by *not* doing what came naturally. She refrained from direct intervention. She admitted to herself that she was too angry to be effective.

EMOTIONAL SUPPORT

Mark, age eleven, was reading a scientific journal in preparation for a school report. He became increasingly upset.

MARK: The whole article is confusing. I can't make head or tail out of it. How does the teacher expect me to write a report when I can't even understand what I am reading?

FATHER: I see you have become aware of how difficult it is to grasp scientific writing. It is often written unclearly.

MARK: That's right. The scientists should learn how to present facts straight.

Mark reread the article and then wrote his report.

The helping ingredient, in this incident, was Father's emotional support. He abstained from defending science or explaining the situation. He avoided criticism and advice such as:

"How come you are always complaining? If you read it more carefully, you would understand it better. It takes intelligence to comprehend a scientific report."

Instead, Father complimented his son for his powers of observation, and sympathized with the difficulty of the task. Mark felt supported enough to risk finishing the report by himself.

ANGER AND ENGLISH

Kim refused to open her reading book. "I hate this book," she protested. "I want to tear it up." Mother took a large piece of paper, folded it, and said, "Make believe this is your reader. Show me what you want to do with it." With obvious relish, Kim tore the paper to pieces and handed them to Mother. Her mother said, "I'm going to write something on each piece. Read it aloud, and sign your name." She wrote, "I hate this book. I detest this book. I despise this book. I denounce this book. I find it repugnant. I find it repulsive. I find it distasteful. I find it nauseating. It is not pleasing. It is not satisfying. It is not enticing. It is not enchanting." Kim read each sentence, laughing hilariously. She signed her name with gusto.

In this episode, Kim's mother motivated her to read and enjoy her reading. She provided Kim security to express her fears and anger. She accepted her daughter as she truly was, and conveyed her acceptance dramatically and artistically.

THE POWER OF ACKNOWLEDGMENT

Stan, age twelve, stormed out of his room yelling at the top of his voice, "It's unfair. My math teacher gave twenty-four long-division problems for homework. I have been working over two hours. And I'm not doing any more. It's a free country, and you can't make me."

What started as a war cry was skillfully turned by Stan's mother into a peace talk. She did not argue with him. Instead, she listened attentivelv and then acknowledged his predicament. She said, "Um-m-m-m, twenty-four long-division problems. Oh-h-h-h, it is grueling and tedious, and it sounds so difficult." The ranting and raving stopped. Stan said, "Look Mom, it's bad, but it's not that bad." He returned to his room and finished his work.

This incident could have easily developed into an all-day quarrel. All that was necessary to spark the fire and start the battle was an unsympathetic comment or a rhetorical question, or a history of the parent's school days. For example:

"How come you're always complaining? If it's not one thing, it's another."

"Why can't you be like your brother? I never have any trouble with him. He does his homework without griping."

"When I was your age, I had ten times more homework than you."

POOR GRADES

Martha, age thirteen, received two unsatisfactory grades on her report card. She quarreled with the teacher about her grades, and came home sad and disgruntled. Usually, her mother would have said, "What did you expect? You got what you deserved. You didn't study enough. You need to spend more time on your homework."

But Mother had learned to be more compassionate. She knew that when someone is drowning, it is not the right time to teach swimming. Mother said, "It makes you feel disappointed." "Yes," agreed Martha, "and discouraged, too." "I know," answered Mother softly.

There was silence for a while, then Martha added, "Next term I'll do better."

Mother related: "In the past, I wouldn't have credited my daughter with caring for her school work. I would have negated her feelings, criticized her conduct, and imputed her motives. I have learned to give my daughter credit for being a responsible and concerned human being."

"A CHALLENGING ASSIGNMENT"

Lawrence, age twelve, a conscientious student, looks upon his homework with dread. It haunts him all afternoon and it robs him of what should be sleeping hours. The ominous cloud darkens his days. He clutches at maps, books, newspapers—to postpone the awful moment. Strangely, once he starts writing, he does his work well.

Mother tried hard to convince him to do his work early and have the evenings free. She begged, explained, and threatened. "It's so easy," she said. "Just sit down and start writing. You know your work. You could do it in no time. It's a cinch for you. So why postpone? You torture yourself needlessly. If you don't change your work habits, I am going to send you away to a boarding school. They will teach you self-discipline."

Nothing helped.

Mother talked over the problem with her son's teacher and changed her approach. Instead of telling Lawrence how easy his homework was, she said, "What a challenging assignment you have today. It seems so complicated and difficult, almost incomprehensible." "Not for me," answered Lawrence. "I am good in arithmetic." Mother replied, "I'll be in the kitchen. Explain it to me when you are finished."

Within one hour, Lawrence was back in the kitchen with his work all done.

On another occasion, Mother said, "I wish you didn't have so much work. I wish you didn't have to work so hard. I wish your evenings were free for enjoyment—reading a novel or watching TV."

"That would be nice," Lawrence answered. "But I do have lots of work. I want to keep my As in math and French."

"What hard-won honors," Mother replied. Lawrence smiled to himself as he started his homework.

NEW WORDS

Mother was preparing dinner. Susan, age thirteen, was doing her homework. "Mom, how do you spell 'contingency' and what does it mean?" she asked. Mother gave the answer. Two minutes later, Susan yelled, "Mom how do you spell 'infinity' and what does it mean?"

Mother was about to explain when she realized that she was being taken. She went to the bookshelf, picked up the dictionary, and handed it to her daughter.

There was a dead silence and a shrug of the shoulders. Susan continued her work by herself. At the dinner table that night, Susan said, "Boy, it was an equinox kind of a day today." Bewildered, Mother said, "What does that mean?" Grinning, Susan said, "Gee, Mom, don't you want to learn a new word? You should look it up in your dictionary."

"You're right," Mother answered. "That's the way to do it." She took out the dictionary and read aloud the meaning of the "new" word.

A NOTE OF TRUTH

Ray, age eight, forgot to do his homework. He asked his mother to invent an excuse for him. Mother refused. She said, "Write a note telling your teacher the truth. I will sign my name next to yours. It will tell the teacher that I understand that sometimes one forgets."

"Thank you very much, Mother," came Ray's reply. He wrote the note, got his mother's signature, and went to school contented.

This incident could have easily been turned into a major battle had his mother used her usual responses: "Why didn't you do the homework? Other children remember. Why do you forget? You are such a scatterbrain. You better shape up!"

Ray's mother has learned that in crises it is best to help rather than preach.

MOTHER LEARNS

Says Mrs. Field: "A notice from school told me that my son Lenny—age sixteen—was failing English. My usual reaction to such news is to let loose a vituperative, acrimonious, and thoroughly destructive cataloguing of all his 'failings' ('You never read a book. You watch too much TV. You don't study enough,' etc.). *His* failure was *my* failure. My disappointment brought on an outburst that demoralized him and me.

"This time, I decided not to indulge in destructive behavior. I asked Lenny's father to help him. When Lenny arrived home from school, I made no allusion to the note. After dinner, Father talked to Lenny quietly, seeking a way to help him over this hurdle. Lenny seemed relieved. He admitted that he had 'goofed up' on homework. He felt sure he could bring his work up to par.

"This was the first time in our family that a dialogue on homework did not deteriorate into a tirade of accusation."

A MOOD OF MUTUALITY

The following short exchange is an example of fruitful communication between parent and teenager about homework.

RAPHAEL (*age seventeen*): I'm going to stay up very late tonight. I've got to finish my report in Social Studies.

FATHER: You still have a lot of work to do before dawn. It must be quite an assignment. How about a supply of coffee to last through the night?

RAPHAEL: Thanks, Dad.

Father related: "In the past, I would have criticized my son: 'Why haven't you finished your report yet? You have been fiddling with it all week. Why do you leave everything for the last moment?' The results were anger and alienation. Now, I see my role is being helpful in discouraging moments."

THE RIGHT HELP

The following dialogue between mother and daughter illustrates parental help that is both gracious and cautious.

ELIZABETH (*age twelve*): Mommy, the class has to write a poem for school. I want mine to be on how you can't tell about a person just by looking at him. But I don't know how to begin.

MOTHER: Hmmm. It's not easy to start a poem, is it?

ELIZABETH: Well . . . I could say "Don't look at me and tell me who I am"—no, wait. I'm going to add, "and in an instant—tell me who I am." Do you think I should say "who" or "what I am?"

MOTHER: Which feels right to you?

ELIZABETH (*pause*): I think "what I am"—and then maybe I could say, "How do you know who I am within my heart? I could be"—now I want to tell some bad things I could be.

MOTHER: Like what?

ELIZABETH: Like—self-centered, cruel, and petty.

MOTHER: Those are powerful words.

ELIZABETH (*writing*): "Or, when you open up the lid to my life . . .

MOTHER: "Open up the lid to my life!" May I borrow your phrase sometime?

ELIZABETH: And now I'd like to tell about the nice things I could be. Oh, I just can't think of the right words. (*Mother is silent.*) I'll look in the thesaurus! (*A minute later she has the book in hand.*) I have them now. "Tender, humane, gracious." And then I want to end with something like "If you get to know me too quickly, you really won't know me that well." Is that good?

MOTHER: The question is not whether it's "good." The question is whether you feel it is poetic; does it express what you want to say?

ELIZABETH: Yes, but is it good?

MOTHER: How do *you* feel about it? You're the artist and must rely on your instinct.

ELIZABETH (*thinking a while*): Well . . . I think I like it better this way. "Take your time to know me, or know me not at all."

MOTHER (*reads the whole poem out loud, then puts her arm around her daughter*): I'm deeply moved by this poem. Please, dear, make a special copy for me.

The poem read:

Don't look at me,
   And in an instant tell me what I am.
How do you know who I am within my heart?
I could be
   Self-centered
   Cruel
   Petty
Or, when you open the lid to my life
You may find me
   Tender
   Humane
   Gracious
Take your time to know me!
Or know me not at all.

                        Elizabeth Cory M.

Mother was helpful because she avoided direct aid. She did not minimize the difficulty of the task ("It's easy if you only start."); nor did she suggest topics, words, and lines. Instead, she listened with attention and responded with admiration. Whenever possible, she encouraged her daughter to rely on her own poetic taste and artistic instincts.

AID: A CHILD'S VIEW

Scott, age ten, had a lot of homework. He struggled with it and found it difficult. He became angry. "I hate my teacher," he yelled. "I am not going to do the homework." "You have to do a tremendous amount of work," his mother acknowledged and said nothing more. Two hours later, after he finished his assignment, Scott said: "Thank you. Mother, for helping me to do my homework." "What do you mean?" his mother asked in surprise. Scott replied: *"You helped me because you didn't make me madder than I was."*

Often, the best help a concerned adult can offer a child is to diminish his anger and defuse his rage.

"A PERSONAL RESPONSIBILITY"

Teachers should not encourage parents to play an overactive role in their children's homework. Homework is the responsibility of the child. When parents take it over, they enter a trap. Homework may become a child's weapon to punish, exploit, and worry his parents. Much misery is avoided when parents show little interest in the minute details of their child's assignments, and instead convey to him clearly: "Homework is for you what work is for us —a personal responsibility."

The main value of homework lies in the experience it gives a child to work on his own. Within limits, it allows him freedom to decide the time and duration of his work. A parent who reminds, nags, and urges vitiates the principal benefit of homework.

Many parents are anxious to help their child with his assignments. There is danger in this help. It may convey to the child: "On your own you are helpless." The best help is indirect—a suitable desk, good lighting, reference books, and no interruptions by errands, conversation, or criticism. Some children work better when they chew a pencil, scratch their heads, or rock their chair. It is best to avoid, at that time, comments on manners of deportment and care of furniture. Critical remarks interfere with mental work. Remaining in the background, parents can give comfort and support rather than voluntary instruction and active assistance. Occasionally, they may clarify a point. Their help is given sparingly but sympathetically. They listen rather than lecture. They show the road but expect the child to reach his destination on his own.

❀ CHAPTER 9

Tales of Motivations

How to Underachieve. Motivating Mottos.

To Reduce Fear. Respect for Process.

"Not a Genius." "Try It, It's Easy."

Abusive Algebra. Need for Autonomy.

Reading Aloud. An Artist Encouraged.

To Motivate Reading.

To Motivate Writing. To Overcome a Fear.

Notes of Appreciation.

Motivation by Identification.

Process and Ethos. A Personal Credo.

HOW TO UNDERACHIEVE

A story is told about a drunk who bumped into a stop sign. Dazed and disoriented, he stepped back and then advanced in the same direction. Once more he hit the sign. He retreated a few steps, waited awhile, and then marched forward. Colliding with the post again, he embraced it in defeat and said: "There is no use. I am fenced in. I am stopped in every direction."

An underachiever is in a similar position: To him every obstacle is a stop sign that cannot be sidestepped—only embraced and leaned on for support. Words of praise fail to motivate an underachiever. In his eyes he is inferior. Anyone who tells him "You are intelligent. You are smart. You can do well" ceases to be an agent of help. The child's logic is: "Only someone stupid or dishonest would say that I am bright." Also doomed to failure are appeals to an underachiever's conscience or pride:

"A boy of your potential and talent."

"You could have the best of everything if you only applied yourself."

"How can you waste such God-given gifts?"

"Do you want to be a bum all your life?"

Children can be lured into learning. They can be tempted and hooked on it; but they cannot be shamed into it. When forced to study, children use their ingenuity to get through school without learning. The following testimonial by a high school student illustrates this point.

"It is easy to 'snow' teachers. If you appear motivated and don't disturb them, they let you live. I became 'school wise' early in the game. I figured out what makes teachers mad: violations of simple rules and 'not trying.' So, I come to school on time, I don't ask troublesome questions, and I am polite. And, of course, I am never caught 'not trying.'

"Our principal stopped me on my way home and asked an original question: 'What did you do in school today?' I was tempted to tell him the truth.

"I apple-polished the English teacher.

"I faked interest in social studies.

"I read comic books during arithmetic.

"I cheated on a science test.

"I did my homework during recess.

"I wrote notes to my girlfriend during Spanish.

"I replied: 'It was a busy day.' He smiled in satisfaction."

In the following dialogue with her music teacher, a sensitive student speaks her mind about what motivates and what blocks learning.

BONNIE (*age eighteen*): My twelve years of schooling have been, for the most part, irrelevant and a waste. Learning to vomit facts and be shrewd in pleasing teachers took the joy out of life. Even in my honors classes, it was mostly a numbers game: accumulate grades, add them up, and divide. Who cares about competing for a number? The essential education was extracurricular: editing the school paper, joining the Debate Society, and taking music lessons.

TEACHER: Your music is important to you.

BONNIE: Yes. It is a part of me. I have to thank you for this. Even when I goof, you don't embarrass me or make me feel like an idiot for making mistakes. That's a cool way to teach.

TEACHER: You like to be told how to improve but without evaluations.

BONNIE: All my life, I've been evaluated and graded. Believe me, I know when I've loused up a lesson or when I've really been with it. I don't need someone to tell me.

MOTIVATING MOTTOS

Teachers often ask psychologists how to motivate children to learn. The answer is "Make it safe for them to risk failure." The major obstacle to learning is fear: fear of failure, fear of criticism, fear of appearing stupid. An effective teacher makes it possible for each child to err with impunity. To remove fear is to invite attempt. To welcome mistakes is to encourage learning.

To motivate learning, one teacher encouraged his class to discuss the meaning of failure in their lives. The children talked about their fear of failure and about the pain of humiliation. As a result of this discussion, the children and the teacher put together a set of motivating mottos to guide life and learning in the classroom. The list was displayed prominently on the front wall.

1. In this class it is permissable to make mistakes.
2. An error is not a terror.
3. Goofs are lessons.
4. You may err, but don't embrace your error. Don't dwell on it, and don't excuse it.
5. Mistakes are for correcting.
6. Value your correction, not your error.
7. Don't let failure go to your head.

TO REDUCE FEAR

During the first school week, one teacher sent a letter to each child in his class. It said: "I have a problem and need your help. I want to encourage all children to answer questions. But I noticed that some children are afraid to do so. They are afraid of being ridiculed. I need your help to make sure that no one is laughed at or made fun of because of a wrong answer. Words and gestures that say or imply 'you are stupid' are forbidden in our class. They hurt feelings and prevent improvement. Instead of attacking another person, say 'I have another answer.' "

The letter, though intended for the children, was also read by their parents. It conveyed to them the teacher's philosophy and reminded them of their own practices. Whenever a child violated this rule, he received a reminder: a copy of this letter.

To free children from fear of incorrect spelling, one teacher told her pupils: "It's difficult to spell unfamiliar words. It would be helpful to me if you'd write the initial consonant of the difficult word with a dash after it. From that clue and the context of your sentence, I'll know which word you need. I'll write it on your paper when I read your work." The children responded by writing many creative stories, poems, and letters.

To reduce fear of tests one school established the following routine: Before an exam, children were supplied with many test questions. The test itself was based on them and on a few new items. The children liked it. Knowing the questions in advance reduced their anxiety. Knowing what to study, they tried harder and retained more.

RESPECT FOR PROCESS

To motivate is to create an atmosphere in which *process* is as important as product.

Six-year-old Newton wrote on the blackboard:

$$8 - 4 = 8$$
$$7 - 3 = 7$$
$$6 - 2 = 6$$

Without a trace of criticism, the teacher said: "Tell me how you arrived at your answers. I'm interested in the *process* of solving problems."

"Here is how I got my answers," explained Newton, demonstrating the process:

Eight take away four is eight $8 - \cancel{4} = 8$
Seven take away three is seven $7 - \cancel{3} = 7$
Six take away two is six $6 - \cancel{2} = 6$

The teacher smiled at the freshness of the explanation. Newton's words gave her a clue to his difficulties: He tended to be literal and needed help in abstracting and symbolizing. The teacher thanked Newton for sharing his thought process with her, before showing him a more conventional method of subtraction.

"NOT A GENIUS"

Parents and teachers sometimes diminish a child's motivation by seemingly benign words. They tell the failing child: "We know you are not a genius, and we don't expect miracles from you. All we want you to do is to work to your capacity. We'll be satisfied if you pass your grade."

These words make it impossible for the child to exert any academic effort. Even if he did his best, he could look forward to nothing but a humiliating "pass." If he failed after trying, it would constitute a public admission of stupidity ("I can't even meet minimal standards."). The child might wisely conclude that there was less risk in not trying.

A more motivating stance signals to children a clear message: "We expect scholarship. Learning is not an accident; it requires effort and determination. We expect it from you."

"TRY IT, IT'S EASY"

On his television show, *The Honeymooners*, Jackie Gleason says to his wife, "You are nothing, Alice. Nothing! I am the boss." "Big deal," answers Alice. "Boss over nothing."

When a child who has difficulties in a subject is told "try it, it's easy" he uses similar logic. "Big deal. Even if I work my hardest, I'll only prove that I can do something easy. But, if I fail, it'll be a real disgrace—an admission that I am stupid and I can't even learn something easy." His final conclusion is, "I can only lose by trying." This principle is illustrated in the following story.

Roger, age eleven, was having difficulty with a math assignment.

ROGER: I guess I am not in the mood for math.
TEACHER: We cannot always do what our moods dictate. I'll explain the problem to you. It's very easy. If you listen carefully, you'll understand it. You are an intelligent boy.

Roger became more distraught. He dropped a book on the floor. When he bent over to pick it up, he toppled the chair.

TEACHER: What's the matter with you? You're not listening. Please concentrate.

ROGER: This problem is too hard.

TEACHER: No, it's not. But I can't help you if your mind is on something else. What are you daydreaming about?

ROGER: I'm not daydreaming. I just don't understand the problem.

TEACHER: You are not listening. It's an easy problem, if you'll only pay attention.

The teacher's pep talk made it impossible for Roger to focus on learning. When a child is told, "You are bright, and the problem is easy" he must defend himself by not listening. His inner logic is, "If I listen and fail to understand, everyone will know that I am dumb." There is less risk in ignoring the teacher: "If I don't try, I can't fail."

Instead of arguing with a child's perception, the teacher can acknowledge it: "It's not easy to do math when one is not in the mood. Perhaps I can be of help." No comments *at all* need to be made about the learner's character or intelligence.

ABUSIVE ALGEBRA

The teacher tried to explain an algebra problem to Ronald. When he did not understand, the teacher became abusive. "I am sorry. That's all I can do for you. It takes intelligence to comprehend algebra." Ronald went back to his seat hurt and angry.

When a child fails to understand our explanation, it is better to attribute it to our approach than to his lack of intelligence. The teacher can save embarrassment by saying, "I have difficulty clarifying this problem. Let's try another approach." Nondefensive and nonaccusing statements motivate children to try their best.

NEED FOR AUTONOMY

Bobby, age ten, said to his teacher, "My parents are going to Europe for a month. Now I'll be able to get my work done."

TEACHER: Now that your parents are away?
BOBBY: Yup—I hate to do anything they tell me to do. Many times I'm ready to practice, then my mother yells out, "Bobby, you haven't practiced yet! It's time for the clarinet." Just because she says it, I don't want to do it. If I practice, I feel I'm doing it for her and not because I want to.
TEACHER: You like to work on your own.
BOBBY: Oh, yes. The same with my homework. I

never feel I'm doing my work because I want
to, but because I'm forced.

TEACHER: You like to feel it is your work and your
decision to do it.

BOBBY: Yes. Now, *for a whole month*, I'll be able to
practice and do my homework without being
reminded.

READING ALOUD

Ramona, a Puerto Rican ten-year-old girl, was
asked to read a few English sentences. She read so
softly, she was barely audible. She stumbled over
many words and finally stopped reading. She put her
book over her face in embarrassment. The teacher
said, "Reading English aloud is not easy. There is
fear of making mistakes and of being laughed at.
It takes courage to stand up and read. Thank you,
Ramona, for trying." The next day, when Ramona
was asked, she stood up and read.

The teacher was helpful because he addressed
himself to Ramona's condition. He showed understanding of her inner reality. He deliberately
avoided unhelpful praise and empty encourage-
ment ("You are dong fine. Read it again, a little

louder. We all make mistakes sometimes, so don't be afraid."). These statements, though well-intentioned, do not motivate.

AN ARTIST ENCOURAGED

Clifford was a talented artist, but he always crumpled or tore up his drawings before he finished them. The teacher knew she had to tread gently, to reach and help Clifford. During a drawing lesson she would pass his desk and say, "That boy really looks like he's running. It's not easy to show action on a drawing paper." Or, "I love the design of that house. I see you are using one of my favorite colors." Or, "I could look at your art for hours."

The grin on Cliff's face would broaden with each comment. The children in the class started noticing his special skill. Cliff enjoyed the attention and admiration, and felt motivated to exhibit his drawings.

TO MOTIVATE READING

Joe's school folder was filled with accounts of misbehavior. He crawled on the floor, wandered around the classroom, hit children, ran out into the hall, etc. He was a big boy, and had been held back because of poor reading. His new teacher had been warned that he would be "difficult."

The teacher made a point of listening to Joe read every day. Her comments were nonjudgmental and appreciative:

> "I enjoyed listening to that story!"
> "Such expressive reading!"
> "Those difficult words were sounded out well!"
> "What an interesting book! I learned a great deal from listening to your reading."

Joe's reading improved. So did his conduct. He became a regular member of the group. The teacher related: "Joe's development of self-esteem seemed to happen right before my eyes."

TO MOTIVATE WRITING

James, age sixteen, handed in a too-short report. Instead of criticizing and admonishing, the teacher wrote, "I found your report interesting, tight, and concise. However, when I finished it, I kept wishing there were more to read." James felt motivated to write longer reports.

TO OVERCOME A FEAR

Diana, age ten, always prepared a delightful project for "Show and Tell" (a stick-puppet, a letter to an author, an original poem, etc.), but she was afraid to stand up in front of the classroom to "share" with her classmates. She would place her project on her desk and admire it, but never volunteer to talk. Her previous teacher tried to minimize her fears by denying her feelings. "Don't be silly, Diana. There is nothing to be afraid of. No one is going to eat you up." Diana resisted and persisted in her silence.

Diana's new teacher had a different approach. She said to Diana, "I enjoyed reading that letter you wrote to Dr. Seuss. I especially liked the sentence about the funny cat in the hat. I wish you would share it with the class." "I'm not standing up *there!*" protested Diana. "It's frightening to stand up and talk to thirty children, I know," replied the teacher. "It's definitely not easy."

After several such exchanges, Diana finally volunteered to share. She was frightened and stiff, but also proud. She began to succeed in other areas, too. Her spelling improved and she began to ask questions during math lessons.

NOTES OF APPRECIATION

Instead of grading papers, one second-grade teacher wrote descriptive notes to the children:

> "Annie, this is neat handwriting."
> "Bob, all your words are spelled correctly."
> "Tommy, the answers on this math paper are all correct."
> "Jo Anne, I love the colors in this drawing."
> "Linda, I see the multiplication is understood."
> "Peter, I was delighted to read such original sentences."

As a result, the children began to write notes to the teacher on the top or bottom of their papers. Examples: "I enjoy handwriting work." "This math is good." "I love spelling tests." The teacher related: "My appreciative notes changed the children's attitude toward written assignments."

MOTIVATION BY IDENTIFICATION

Jennifer, age thirteen, was a reluctant piano player. She resisted her lessons and refused to practice. Her attitude changed drastically when a new teacher was engaged.

Jennifer herself explained the change in her motivation and behavior:

"My first teacher was insensitive. 'Where is your mind right now?' she used to yell. 'If you don't concentrate, you'll never learn to play. You have sloppy hands as it is.' Can you imagine a teacher talking like that?

"Since I started studying with my new teacher, I have improved a lot. She is unbelievable. For instance, I played 'Rhapsody in Blue' incorrectly and in wrong timing. Mrs. S. said to me, 'I really enjoyed your rendition. Your interpretation was so original and creative. Now let me show you how it was intended to be played.' Then she sat down and played it correctly. It was the most gentle criticism I ever heard. I thought to myself: 'What a teacher.' "

PROCESS AND ETHOS

The vignettes in this chapter stress the importance of process in education and motivation. The teacher's response is considered crucial to the child's learning. Recent school disruptions, however, indicate that congruent communication, though necessary, is not a sufficient condition for learning. Bel Kaufman, author of *Up the Down Staircase* (1965), returned to school for a teaching stint in 1971. She was shocked by the changes in mood and conduct: muggings in the hall, dope on the stairs, robbery at knife point, extortion, assaults, and rape. "In the old days, no matter how 'difficult' some schools were there was the hum of work and the sense of achievement. In spite of dullness, waste, and ineptitude, teaching was going on and learning. One knew where one was. Teachers were overworked then but not frightened. Administration was pompous but not paranoid, kids were 'disruptive' but not criminals." Kaufman's conclusion was sad and clear: "For this generation of angry urban children our traditional schools are obsolete." (*McCall's* magazine, February 1972.)

In schools with an anti-learning atmosphere, the class ethos warns students: "Don't cooperate. Don't volunteer. Don't collaborate with the teacher. Don't participate in his projects. Don't finish assignments, and don't do homework." In such a school a child may underachieve to avoid class censure. He may risk scholastic failure to avert social doom. Though he may privately prefer learning, he takes his cue from the active anti-intellectuals, the aggressive advocates of disruption. Unless a drastic change is effected in atmosphere and ethos, teaching and learning in such schools becomes impossible.

A PERSONAL CREDO

My views on motivation are best summed up in the following tale:

A fire broke out in a cramped attic. The firemen who rushed to the rescue found a man heavily asleep. They tried to carry him down the stairs but could not, and they despaired of saving him. Then the chief arrived and said: "Wake him up and he'll save himself."

The moral of the story is clear. Children bored and asleep will not be affected by a well-intentioned rescuer. They need to be awakened to their potential, and they will save themselves.

CHAPTER 10

Helpful Procedures and Practices

To Touch Life in the Classroom.

Who Asks the Questions?

The Listening Game.

To Suspend Judgment.

Letters of Consequence. Resource Directory.

Underachievers as Tutors. Paired Learning.

Student Involvement Programs.

Parents in School. Teacher's Aides.

Practical Innovations.

TO TOUCH LIFE IN THE CLASSROOM

Teachers are suspicious of innovations, and with good reason. "Year after year new programs are introduced in the schools. To the public each program may signify an educational advance; for the teacher . . . it is more likely to be a replay of an old tune . . . a game of educational musical chairs, in which each district hails as new and innovative that which is being discarded as a failure in a neighboring area." (Albert Shanker, *The New York Times*, July 18, 1971)

Innovations geared to upgrade education, especially in ghetto schools, have had limited effectiveness. One cynical critic explained: "When methods that failed in middle-class elementary schools are introduced to ghetto nursery schools, they do not bring success. They bring disaster. It takes a child about three years of schooling to become convinced that he is dumb. Now, with the help of the Federal government, he can learn it in kindergarten."

Innovations based on belief in the magic of quantity (more money, more teachers, more services) have not lived up to their promise. What children need and what only teachers can provide is quality of instruction and equality of dignity. The procedures and practices depicted in this chapter are neither flamboyant nor world-shaking, but they enhance the quality of life in the classroom.

WHO ASKS THE QUESTIONS?

The conventional classroom is contrived and illogical in its main method: Teachers, who know the subject, ask questions of children, who do not know it. To undo this tedious tradition, some schools have reversed this absurd order. From first grade on, children are taught to raise questions. The search for them constitutes an integral part of studying. In the beginning, the emphasis is on the number of questions children can formulate. Later the quality of the question is examined.

To motivate children to pose questions one teacher* introduced a game: He brought to class a black attaché case and told his students that it

* Frank Miceli, "Education and Reality," in *Teaching as a Subversive Activity* by Neil Postman and Charles Weingartner (New York: Delacorte Press. 1969), p. 172.

had a small computer able to answer any question. "What question," he asked, "do you want it to answer?" Dozens of questions came:

"When was I born?"
"What is my mother's maiden name?"
"What should we do about Vietnam?"
"Why are grownups always angry at teenagers?"
"Why can't we grade ourselves at school?"
"If everyone makes H-bombs, won't someone drop one some day?"
"If love is dead, why do I feel so great with my boyfriend?"
"How many miles from St. Croix to San Francisco?"

The teacher then told the class that the computer was too expensive to use for questions with already known answers. The students examined their list and eliminated such questions (e.g., When was I born?). Next the teacher disclosed that the computer had trouble with vague questions. For example: In the question, "What should we do about Vietnam?" what is meant by "we"? What is meant by "should"? Is it a "moral should"? Is it a "political should"? In the question, "How many miles from St. Croix to San Francisco?" what is meant by "miles"? Air miles? Ship miles? The students soon realized that there was no miraculous computer in the case. But they continued to play "the black attaché" game and insisted that the case be physically present at every session.

THE LISTENING GAME

To teach listening one school instituted this practice: One hour, every other day, students engage in a discussion of personal and social issues about which they feel strongly. One unusual rule is observed: Before a person has his say, he must restate the gist of the previous speaker's words to his satisfaction. This rule is not as simple as it sounds. It is the heart of congruent communication. It requires each speaker to focus on another's words and feelings, to enter his frame of mind and to understand his point of view. Strange changes occur in the children and their teachers as they go through this procedure: They talk less, listen more, and gain in empathic understanding.

TO SUSPEND JUDGMENT

A teacher's judgmental statements impede a child's learning. To reduce the number of such statements, one school used this procedure: Each teacher was asked to keep track of the number of adjectives he attached to students during one day, every week. Since the aim was to induce teachers to suspend judgments, both negative and positive evaluations were tallied. The tallying was done by the teacher himself, or by a monitor assigned by him. Some teachers used tape recorders. Teachers became conscious of how much their language was sprinkled with judgmental adjectives such as: right, wrong, good, bad, smart, stupid, neat, sloppy, bright, dumb, pretty, ugly, etc. Two teachers who taped their lessons reported the following agonizing appraisal:

"I was surprised to hear all the hurting words I say to pupils, despite my good intentions. I wanted to shut off the recorder. I heard words foreign to my philosophy. One tape was enough to shock me into a humbler vision of myself as an educator, and to a revision of my tactics as a teacher.

"After listening to myself for an hour, I got depressed. I could not believe it was me: The sarcastic tone, the harsh voice, the biting comments. I decided to re-examine the quality of my communication with children, to pinpoint the small sins, the insults by implication, the odious comparisons, the faint praise, the judgmental tone."

LETTERS OF CONSEQUENCE

To reduce children's inner irritation one school introduced this innovation: Every morning children were asked to write a letter to the teacher about anything or anyone who angered them lately. They were free to write anything they wanted. The method helped teachers to keep in touch with children's feelings, to prevent explosions, and to render emotional first aid.

One teacher gave up assigning compositions to his students. Instead he invited them to write him letters on any subject they felt strongly about. Their notes were considered personal. His reply was detailed.

These personal communications had a profound impact on the students. In their letters they explored their fear of social rejection, the frailty of friendship, sexual ventures, religion and morals, money matters, personality and character, and future plans of work and education. Interestingly, though never corrected, the grammar and spelling of the students improved.

RESOURCE DIRECTORY

To highlight the varied abilities of different children, one teacher compiled a directory of "Who Is Good in What in Our Class." Anyone needing help in solving algebra problems, shooting baskets in the gym, or building a boat could use the directory to find his "tutor." The resource directory encouraged mutual assistance and helped change the distribution of prestige and influence in the classroom.

UNDERACHIEVERS AS TUTORS

Underachievers improve when they have the opportunity to tutor. A sixth-grader with reading difficulties is able to reach and teach younger children with similar troubles. He understands his student's soft spots and is patient and compassionate. In the process of helping, the helper is helped most. He is motivated to do his best, and he himself learns to read. He also has the ennobling experience of feeling needed and being useful.

A team of social scientists from the University of Michigan under the leadership of Ronald and

Peggy Lippit has been testing different methods of training student tutors. The experiments were conducted in Detroit's suburban and inner-city schools. In one experiment thirty high school volunteers acted as academic aides to junior high school students. Thirty junior high school students worked in elementary schools, and thirty fifth- and sixth-graders tutored in the first and second grades. They helped in reading, writing, spelling, math, physical education, shop, and field trips.

The tutors received in-service training in weekly seminars. They listened to tapes of experienced tutors, became aware of different learning problems, and learned techniques of communicating with younger children. Each helper also conferred with the teacher of the children he tutored. Results showed that in the process of helping others to learn, tutors acquired social skills and academic competence. They learned to relate to younger children and to fill gaps in their own studies. As one teacher put it: "The children return from the helping session with an increased will to do their own work. The program has increased their self-respect and belief in their own ability."

Ronald and Peggy Lippit report that "The younger children gain considerably from participating in a cross-age helper program. From their helpers they acquire an incentive to work through to success instead of quitting. . . . Older students . . .

care. They are companions in games that teach skills. They help meet the younger children's needs to feel successful and important." Teachers report that tutored children "show increased self-respect, self-confidence, and pride in their progress."*

PAIRED LEARNING

In some schools children are allowed to form partnerships. Two children do their homework together, take tests together, and share the same marks. Results show that children working in pairs do better work than either child has done before. This strategy is especially helpful to underachievers. They give up the defense of deliberate failure, which they have used to protect self-esteem. In a partnership they take risks and experience success. In paired learning each child assumes the role of both teacher and learner, giver and receiver. Each can check his performance without fear and correct his errors without penalty.

* Ronald Lippit and Peggy Lippit, "Cross-Age Helpers," in *NEA Journal*, March 1968.

STUDENT INVOLVEMENT PROGRAMS

Many schools have recognized the students' right to participate in the operation of their institution. In one school a student advisory committee meets with the principal every week to present him with ideas about curriculum, activities, and problems affecting student life. The principal uses these meetings to inform students on current issues and to consult with them on future plans. One committee member related, "We feel we are individually influencing our education, and that we now have a voice in what is happening in our school."

In one school students set up "an ideal school district." They appointed a student faculty, administration, school board, and superintendent. Each appointee studied how his role was played in reality. After six months of study and research, the students presented their findings and conclusions to the parents, teachers, and community. They recommended:

1. That teachers be allowed more freedom in *how* to teach their courses.
2. More application of course content to man and society.
3. More discussions, reading, and writing rather than memorizing, testing, and factual reports.
4. More active participation on the part of

students in dialogue with teachers; more student panels; use of students as lecturers and discussion leaders.

5. One-to-one conferences between student and teacher for purposes of evaluation and constructive criticism.

PARENTS IN SCHOOL

One private elementary school encouraged parents to attend their children's classes one day a month to serve as teacher's aides. The results were fruitful. The parents witnessed, first hand, some of the difficulties involved in teaching a large group of children. As a result parents' attitudes toward teachers changed for the better. The children liked having parents in school. The teachers were more motivated to prepare their lessons at home, to talk less in class, and to avoid unnecessary conflicts.

TEACHER'S AIDES

The demands of daily life in the classroom can destroy teaching. To cope with all the routine details is to be devoured by them. An elementary school teacher engages in more than one thousand interpersonal exchanges every day. Even when they are pleasant, they are tiring. When they occur at a rushed pace in the tense atmosphere of a classroom, they drain the teacher's energy. Here is a sample of fifty statements made by one teacher during her first fifteen minutes of instruction.

> "Line up with your class."
> "Stand up tall."
> "Take your neighbor's hand."
> "Don't drop your books."
> "Class, forward."
> "Pick up your feet."
> "Follow your class."
> "Open the classroom door."
> "The last child in, close the door."
> "Boys, go to your seats."
> "Girls, go to your seats."
> "Take chairs off desks."
> "Boys, hang up your coats."
> "Girls, hang up your coats."
> "Cloak room monitor, close the doors."
> "Put away your lunch boxes."
> "Stand up for flag salute."
> "Flag monitor, come forward."
> "Class, sit down."
> "Clear off your desks."
> "Take out your homework."

"Girls, sharpen your pencils."

"Boys, sharpen your pencils."

"Pass your papers forward."

"Attendance monitor, take attendance."

"Plant monitor, water the plants."

"Joseph, feed the gerbils."

"Children, listen to the announcements on the loud-speaker."

"Jeffrey, take the attendance to the office."

"Line up for bathroom before reading."

"Get ready for reading."

"Go to your reading group."

"Groups one and two do the assignment on the board."

"Group three go to the back of the room."

"Turn to page thirty-four."

"Sit up straight."

"Don't kick your neighbor."

"Keep your reader on your lap."

"Don't lose your place."

"Read to yourself."

"Now, read aloud."

"Janet, stop hitting Michael."

"Doris, don't daydream. Start reading."

"Jimmy, pay attention to your lesson."

"John, turn to the right page."

"Nora, blow your nose."

"Nora, get a tissue. Don't use your sleeve."

"George, lower your voice."

"George, return to your seat."
"Please quiet down."

Many schools have increased their teachers' effectiveness by freeing them from clerical and housekeeping tasks. All noninstructional chores are done by teacher's aides. They, with the help of student monitors,

Take attendance.

Collect milk money, lunch money, and seed money.

Distribute milk, straws, and crackers.

Open and close classroom doors and windows.

Adjust shades.

Switch lights on and off, when necessary.

Maintain order in clothes closet.

Keep blackboard and erasers clean.

Keep paper supply stocked and in order.

Distribute and collect pencils and crayons.

Distribute and collect workbooks.

Give back the corrected papers.

Keep science table in order.

Keep library table in order.

Keep art table in order (restoc.. paper, mix paints, clean tools.)

Water plants and flowers.

Feed birds, animals, or fish.

Clean cages and aquariums.

Keep phonograph and records in working order.

Obtain and thread projector, show and rewind films,˙ and return projector to audiovisual room.

Distribute and collect games for indoor activities during bad weather.

Answer telephone when teacher is busy.

Supervise flag saluting exercise.

Send out P.T.A. notices.

Receive and greet visitors to the classroom.

Help orient new students to school routine.

Maintain bulletin board: store pictures, pins, and paper in proper files.

Carry out errands.

Take inventory of textbooks.

Collect Red Cross donations.

Give out lunch cards.

Conduct daily health and appearance checks.

Keep health records.

Collect clothes and articles for P.T.A. bazaars.

Renew bus passes.

Check library books.

Teacher's aides and student monitors are capable of taking care of these routine assignments satisfactorily. Some aides also tutor students individually and in small groups. They save the teacher time and energy and create favorable conditions for teaching and learning.

PRACTICAL INNOVATIONS

This chapter describes practices and procedures that enhance classroom life and learning without demanding revolutionary changes in school personnel or budget. Many of them can be introduced by a single teacher; others by a single school. All the innovations are practical and can be initiated at any time. These procedures free teachers from energy-depleting chores, augment students' sense of personal potency and improve communication between teacher and child.

CHAPTER 11

Adult Encounters

In Conference: Optimal Conditions;
Impertinent Assumptions; Advice;
A Helpful Dialogue; To Assuage Anger;
Notes of Hope; To Close a Conference.
Troubles with Administrators:
Professional Conduct; "Expository Notes";
No Place for Rebukes; Destructive Help;
Gracious Instructions;
"I Cannot Deal with Sarcasm";
Coping with Authority;
Coping with Unsolicited Advice;
"13 Rules for Administrators Who Wish To
Subvert Teaching."
Spontaneity, Not Impulsivity.

This chapter deals with the adults who educate the child: parents, teachers, administrators. It tells of their encounters with each other in conference and conflict. The emphasis is on communication. Like a foreign language, helpful communication, once acquired, can be readily applied in daily life. It provides a healing touch in times of trouble. It assuages anger, diminishes dissension, and supports sanity.

IN CONFERENCE

When a teacher talks to parents about their children, he inevitably intrudes on family dreams. To his parents a child may represent their last hope for a better future. Through him they may still dream of gaining affluence, honors, escape from anonymity, and a place in society. What the teacher says about the child touches on deep feelings and hidden fantasies. A concerned teacher is aware of the impact of his words. He consciously avoids comments that may casually kill dreams.

OPTIMAL CONDITIONS

What are optimal conditions for a parent-teacher conference? A quiet corner, protection from interruptions and a teacher who listens. The words exchanged during the conference may be forgotten, but the mood of the meeting will linger on. It will decide the subsequent attitudes and actions of the parents. Nothing spoils the mood of a conference more than interruptions by phone, secretary, or colleague. It tells the waiting parent: "You are not important. I have more urgent matters to attend to." The telephone can wait, and a sign on the door, "In conference," may keep out most people. Those who will insist on "just a minute" with us can be told "I'll see you as soon as I am free."

IMPERTINENT ASSUMPTIONS

Some teachers tend to talk about themselves during parent conferences. They discuss their personal experience, implying that it can serve as a model for others. A parent may resent this assumption. "I am not you," a mother may say to herself. "My situation is different. If you understood it, you would not talk like that." Even when directly asked by a parent, "What would you do in my position?" a teacher will show respect for another person's uniqueness by not assuming his place too readily. It is possible to draw on one's experience indirectly: "Some people have found it helpful to . . . But how does it seem to you? Does it make sense in your situation?" The teacher shuns statements such as, "I know how you feel. If I were in your place I would . . ." Such presumption provokes resistance. The parent may proceed to prove to the teacher that he does not really understand the situation.

A teacher does not preach to parents. Moralizing is demoralizing. It arouses anxiety and resentment, stops honest self-expression, and invites pretense. Example:

TEACHER: Can't you find half an hour a day to help your child with his homework? It's your child, and he won't be a child forever.
PARENT: I'll try. But I don't know when I'll find the time. I am a working mother.
TEACHER: For the sake of your child I know you'll find the time.

It is not a teacher's role to arouse anxiety and evoke guilt.

ADVICE

People often seek advice only to prove to the giver that it is worthless. When a parent asks for direct advice, a teacher may choose not to comply with the request. The best advice about advice was given by an experienced teacher: "Whenever possible, I avoid telling parents what to do and what not to do. Even when they ask for it, I postpone giving instant advice. I try to find out what they think about the situation and what alternatives they have considered. I encourage them to talk about their fears and hopes and to risk stating opinions and making decisions." At best a parent can benefit from advice only after he has done "emotional homework"; after he has expressed himself sufficiently and been understood empathically. When accepted with respect and understanding, the parents themselves often suggest the advice they have been trying to solicit from the teacher. One teacher related: "My advice to parents is always tentative. I never urge or cajole. I suggest and ask for their reactions. I try to put into words their expectations and doubts."

A HELPFUL DIALOGUE

The following dialogue is an example of helpful exchange between parent and teacher:

MRS. ADAMS: My Debbie has been accepted for an Intellectually Gifted Children's class in the fall. We're very excited, but it means she'll have to travel.

TEACHER: Oh . . .

MRS. ADAMS: Do you think we should send her?

TEACHER: What are your feelings?

MRS. ADAMS: I don't know how Debbie will feel in a new school.

TEACHER: You're concerned about her adjustment? How does Debbie feel about it?

MRS. ADAMS: We haven't told her. Her father thinks she'll get a swelled head if she knows. Do you think we should send her?

TEACHER: Tell me, what are your options?

MRS. ADAMS: If she stays at her present school, she'll be in a regular class and we won't be able to transfer her.

TEACHER: If she goes to the gifted class, could she come back to this school if she's not satisfied?

MRS. ADAMS: Yes, she could do that. (*Pause*) Do you think we should tell Debbie? Would she get a swelled head?

TEACHER: It's such a pleasure for a child to hear good news about herself.

MRS. ADAMS: I will tell her. Thanks so much. You were a great help.

To Assuage Anger

In the following incident, a teacher helped a mother get over her angry feelings toward school.

Pearl's mother arrived in school fuming. At great length she explained that her daughter had been insulted by the gym teacher. Pearl's regular teacher listened to Mother's story without interruption, then said: "What a hard day you had." "Yes," said Mother. "I didn't need additional aggravation." The teacher said, "It's hard enough taking care of three active children and working full time, but this really added insult to injury." "Yes," said Mother. "Pearl is such a gentle child. She likes your class very much. That's why she was never absent this year." "It's a pleasure to have her in my class," replied the teacher. "And I am so glad we had a chance to meet."

This teacher was helpful, because she avoided fruitless inquiries about who said what to whom. Instead, she gave emotional first aid to the upset mother. She listened to her words and reflected her mood. When Mother felt accepted and understood, her anger evaporated.

NOTES OF HOPE

Parents often ask a teacher, "What's wrong with my child?" A sophisticated teacher does not answer such questions. He does not say, "Well, since you asked, let me tell you. Your son is lazy, sloppy, disobedient, and irresponsible." Or, "Your daughter is shy, insecure, and a poor sport." A teacher never talks in adjectives. He does not list and label traits of personality and character. Neither does he focus on past misdeeds: "Jimmy never comes to school on time. He does not do his homework. His notebooks are messy and he fights continuously." Instead, a helpful teacher concretely describes areas in need of improvement.

"Jimmy needs improvement in coming to school on time, doing his arithmetic at home, keeping his notebooks neat, and learning to settle arguments in words."

When Al's mother returned from her interview with his teacher, Al, age twelve, asked her, "What did the teacher tell you about me?" His mother replied, "I wrote down what she said. You may read it, if you want to." Al, who expected familiar remarks about misbehavior and homework, was surprised when he read, "Al needs improvement in seeing himself as a responsible person, worthy of respect and capable of doing his work."

Not only Al, but his mother too, benefited from this note. It turned her mind toward future improvement rather than past faults. It avoided blame and despair ("Al is irresponsible. He does not do his work, and may fail his grade."). It gave direction and hope.

Every teacher-parent interview can end on such a constructive note. Examples:

"Bill needs improvement in considering himself a person able to study independently and worthy of appreciation."

"Celia needs improvement in viewing herself as a person who can contribute to class discussions and be good company to friends."

"Dave needs improvement in taking joy in learning, talking more freely, and sharing his knowledge with others."

"Eva needs improvement in thinking of herself as a future scholar who has long-lived interests, and who sees tasks through to completion."

"Francine needs improvement in picturing herself as a person who can work without interruptions, talk more politely and resolve arguments peacefully."

"Gladys needs improvement in learning to express her anger without insult."

"Harold needs improvement in trusting his own feelings and in thinking well of himself."

To Close A Conference

It is not easy to close a conference with some parents. They may continue to talk beyond the allotted time and often bring up new material on their way to the door. The teacher feels caught in a vise: He may be late for another appointment or fearful of missing his bus. But there he stands politely, seething inside. It is the teacher's task to indicate that closing time is approaching: "I see our time is about up. Is there anything else you'd like to add at this point?" If a parent needs more time to discuss a new issue, it is best to suggest another appointment. "Mrs. Jones, could we meet again or take it up on the phone? I can't listen well right now. I am worried about missing my bus." The closing phase of a conference should provide time for gracious separation. Care must be taken not to spoil a good conference at the last minute by sudden severance and abrupt eviction.

TROUBLES WITH ADMINISTRATORS

To many teachers the principal or his assistant is the cutting edge of the school bureaucracy. They see him as the person who often makes their lives miserable by tactless intrusions and petty demands. The vignettes in this section tell of edgy encounters between teachers and administrators and of the methods teachers use to protect their dignity.

PROFESSIONAL CONDUCT

This episode was related by a young substitute teacher:

"Last Friday I was given the worst assignment in school: the bottom sixth-grade class. I faced fourteen lunatics and talked to the walls! Half of them were in and out of the room. The screaming and yelling was beyond endurance. No assistance came from anyone. Finally, I threw up my hands. My voice was gone. My legs felt weak. Then the assistant principal appeared at the door and started to insult me in front of the class. He said, 'You certainly have a talent for lousing up things. If you gave them work to do, instead of relaxing, perhaps you would have order in the room. Why aren't they working? What are you here for?'

"I was dumbfounded and mortified."

In this incident, the assistant principal violated basic professional standards. A professional knows how to behave, even when he does not know what to do. He knows that when things go wrong, first aid, not criticism, is needed. A teacher drowning in noise needs not advice, but instant help. The A.P. could have taken over the class for a while, providing the teacher with a brief respite. All good advice could have waited for a private time and place.

"Expository Notes"

The first-grade teacher sent a note to the A.P. requesting pencils. The A.P. wrote back: "I have no pencils. Furthermore, considering the fact that you have a class in front of you, how do you have time to write expository notes?"

The teacher scribbled back: "It's difficult, but I manage. Can you manage to get us pencils? This hard-working class will appreciate your efforts, and I will stop writing you notes."

No Place for Rebukes

This incident was related by a second-grade teacher:

"The principal reprimanded me in front of my class about a minor assignment that had slipped my memory. I became angry. But instead of blowing my top, I said firmly, 'This is not the time to discuss this matter.' The principal backed down. 'I shall see you privately,' he said.

"I felt relieved and reassured in my capacity to cope with authority figures. I felt an inner strength and I liked myself. I was glad that I kept my cool, that I neither folded in fear nor melted in apologies. I held my ground with strength and dignity."

DESTRUCTIVE HELP

Mrs. Z., a substitute teacher, arrived at school half an hour late. The principal was waiting for her. In front of the children he asked, "Why were you late?" "I'll tell you later," replied Mrs. Z., diplomatically avoiding a trap.

What she could not avoid was his "help." Before he left he said, "If you have any trouble with this class, call me." He then turned to one boy in the back of the class and shouted, "José, if you give Mrs. Z. any trouble whatsoever, you'll be sorry. I'll see to it myself." He then addressed the whole class· "Children, I want you to be good today. Remember, and don't forget."

A principal needs to be aware of the implications of his words. To warn children to be good means, "I don't expect you to behave well." To tell a teacher, "If they give you trouble, call me" means, "I don't have faith in your ability to handle this class." To ask a teacher for her reasons for being late means, "I don't believe you have a legitimate excuse." A person in authority must be sensitive to his impact on other human beings.

GRACIOUS INSTRUCTIONS

A teacher was substituting in a first-grade class. The assistant principal walked in and looked over the desk.

A.P.: Where is the experience chart for discussing the date and weather?

TEACHER: I used this calendar. We discussed the date and I drew an umbrella to symbolize the rain.

A.P.: You must use an experience chart. Considering you have an Early Childhood Science license, you should know to do it.

TEACHER: I don't think it's the time to discuss it now. I'll be available at noon if you'd like to talk about it further.

A.P.: That won't be necessary.

Instructions are heeded better when given succinctly. They are appreciated more when offered without arousing shame or guilt. The A.P. could have told the teacher in one discreet sentence to use the experience chart for dates and weather. No discussion was necessary.

"I CANNOT DEAL WITH SARCASM"

The second-grade teacher sent a note to the principal. "Please let me know when four of my children could present in the auditorium a five-minute play they have written. Thank you for your attention."

She received the following reply: "Dear Mrs. R.: You may have the assembly program on the 4th of July."

On the same note, the teacher answered, "I cannot deal with sarcasm. Please look at your calendar and let me know when I can use the auditorium. Thank you."

The principal sent another note: "I will not permit you to hog the auditorium. You have already presented a production once."

On the same sheet of paper, the teacher answered, "I hardly think that five minutes of assembly time is tantamount to hogging the auditorium. Please check your calendar and let me know when I can have the five minutes. I appreciate the lack of sarcasm this time."

The following week, the principal found a five-minute spot for the production.

COPING WITH AUTHORITY

This incident was related by a young teacher:

"A monitor appeared at my door and told me that the principal wanted to see me urgently. In the office, I found an angry man, waving a letter at me. 'Because of you, a student was expelled,' he said. 'You did not properly prepare your children for third grade. You failed them by not disciplining them enough.' I did not lose my temper. I just said, 'It sounds like something's happened.' The gory details followed. Adele and Nancy had been fooling around. Their teacher, Miss S., got angry, yelled at the girls, and sent them out of the room. Later Miss S. demanded an apology. Nancy complied readily, but Adele handed in the following note:

> Dear Miss S.,
>   It has come to my attention that you do not understand children. I do not like to be yelled at.
>
>   Sincerely,
>   Adele

"Miss S. exploded. She read the note to the class and ordered Adele to the office. She was told to bring her mother to school.

"The verdict was severe: Adele was placed in another school. The principal held me responsible. In my class, such notes were not only permissible but heartily approved. I felt bad—until I realized a few facts.

"1. Little Adele had dealt with her feelings in a sophisticated way.

"2. She had written a well-constructed, perfectly spelled letter, quite similar to letters I had sent to many children.

"3. Adele may have been ousted from school, but she had maintained her integrity.

"I felt better."

COPING WITH UNSOLICITED ADVICE

The assistant principal heard Mrs. K. discussing a problem with the children. When he saw her at lunch, he said, "I didn't care for the way you had handled the situation."

"You would have handled it differently?" Mrs. K. replied.

"You were too easy with them. Children have to learn to take disappointments in their stride," the A.P. asserted.

"Wait," Mrs. K. said, taking out her notebook, "let me jot this down."

"You're always writing things down," he said. "I can't think while you write."

"It helps me to remember what you've said if I write it down," Mrs. K. assured.

"Oh," he said, "I didn't know you took the time to reread what I've said to you. That's very gratifying."

"13 RULES FOR ADMINISTRATORS WHO WISH TO SUBVERT TEACHING"

This is the title of a tongue-in-cheek article published in a journal of the American Federation of Teachers (*Changing Education*, Spring, 1968). The author, William H. Boyer, ironically summarizes all that is wrong between teachers and administrators.

These rules will not be of value to all administrators, only to those who aspire to subvert effective teaching but are not successful because they lack understanding of the necessary procedures. . . .

1. Let the teacher know, as soon as possible, that the administrator is the policy maker. If the teacher questions this principle, use the Aristotelian argument. Explain that the "essence" of administration is to make policy, not simply to administer policy—that the "nature" of administration is policy making. Show that this conclusion followed from an analysis of the concept of administration. If the teacher's rational faculty is so weak that this basic truth is not apparent, the "law of exercise" can be used, and the statement THE AD-

MINISTRATION DECIDES POLICY can be repeated until the image is sufficiently stamped in.

2. Let the teacher know that he is a member of a team, and that if he "plays ball" he'll get along well. Administrators who feel fatherly sometimes prefer the metaphor "the family" instead of "the team." This metaphor has more atavistic appeal, but it opens one to some embarrassment if there is a request for designation of the role of the mother. The problem is equally awkward if the administrator is a woman, so "the team" with its neuter gender is increasingly preferred by enlightened subverters.

3. If a teacher fails to conform, always defend your actions against him on the principle that it is necessary for the good of the profession. If he is audacious enough to question this principle, be prepared with the ultimate argument—let him know that he or any other individual teacher is dispensable, it is only the profession which is indispensable. Teachers come and go, but the profession lives forever.

4. Explain that the purpose of ₋ne school is to serve the community. Indicate the way in which you want the teacher to serve the community, and make it clear that to offend the beliefs of prominent members of the community in no way serves this objective.

5. Let the teacher know that his first obligation, even in his private life, is to the school. If a teacher claims he has contracted his professional services but has not sold his life, tell him you are not interested in "semantic" arguments.

6. Remind all teachers that educational institutions are like industry and must be run by those

in control. A teacher therefore cannot be independent, he can only be for or against the administration. Groups which exclude administrators cannot be tolerated. Such activity could result in collective opposition to the administration and therefore pose a threat to the stability of the school. Such conflict is obviously not in the best interests of the profession.

7. Do not tolerate teacher requests to participate in curriculum development. If there is any question of authority, use the Aristotelian argument again, and explain that only the administrator has the "broad view" of things or else he would not be an administrator.

8. When there is conflict between educational objectives and administrative expediency, the latter must supersede. This principle results in greater organizational efficiency, and its special justification lies in the fact that administrators understand public relations and finance, and these are both the means and the ends of the institution. A teacher who fails to adjust to these basic principles of education should be discharged as soon as possible. It is imperative that he not be given tenure.

9. Faculty meetings should be held periodically to provide opportunity for a democratic discussion of the problems of the school. Remember those who disagree with the administration, for it is necessary that faculty who are disloyal be identified and weeded out.

10. Do not let teachers become influential in problems of hiring, firing, or promotion. This rule can be justified on the basis of the self-evident principle that an organization cannot be well run

if authority is divided. Or one might refer to the adage that "too many cooks spoil the broth."

11. If the question of academic freedom arises, assure the teacher that there is ample academic freedom. (Avoid the mistake of having a policy statement in writing.) If the details of such freedom are requested, indicate your sincerity through a friendly smile, and assure him that no one who has done what he is paid to do has ever had his freedom restricted.

12. Reward the loyalty of senior teachers through free periods and small classes in their chosen subjects and give them selected diligent and compliant students. The beginning teacher is best disciplined to the realities of the profession through a full schedule of large classes loaded with discipline problems in a subject field outside his area of preparation.

13. Help teachers enjoy democratic rites by dividing issues into those that are important and those that are trivial. Give the latter type to the teachers, and explain that it is not the problem but the process which is important. It is especially stimulating to offer this kind of ceremonial catharsis with the onset of spring.

Teachers, intimately familiar with these rules, are no longer willing to be intimidated by them. They demand their fair share in deciding school policy and procedure. Plato said that the essence of slavery lay in separating the forming of purposes from their execution, and lodging them in separate persons. Teachers are determined to abolish such anachronistic attitudes and policies in school administration.

SPONTANEITY, NOT IMPULSIVITY

In my seminars I am often asked by a teacher or principal: "Can I never be myself in talking to children, parents, or colleagues? Must I always stop and think what to say and what not to say? Isn't it contrived and lacking in spontaneity?"

An adult needs to examine his natural reactions to children and peers, to separate the chaff from the wheat, to learn what helps and what hurts. Mental hospitals are full of patients who, as children, were given the "spontaneous treatment" by their parents. "What was on their lungs was on their tongues," and their tongues spewed invective and insult. I am for spontaneity. I am against impulsivity masquerading as spontaneity.

A competent educator, like an accomplished musician, devotes years and effort to acquiring techniques. Once acquired, they are unseen. The violinist plays his music as though problems of fingering, bowing and double stopping never existed. A principal, a teacher, or a parent can respond helpfully, as though congruent communication were his native tongue.

CHAPTER 12

Students Recall Their Teachers

"How Is the Vacuum of Your Mind?"

The Value of Zero. Echoes of Events.

The Nazi. Drama and Life.

"Time to Know Us." Concise Contempt.

The Core Truth. Overconcern. Trust.

Lessons in Filibuster.

Lessons in Indifference. "Hurry Slowly."

"Too Good for the Common People."

A Sense of Mystery. Harvest of Hate.

Programmed Robot. A Magic Touch.

Magnetic Fields. No Exit. Golden Tongue.

An Autobiography. Reverence for Life.

Verbal Parsimony. At Home in the World.

A Poem to a Teacher.

Teachers have a unique opportunity to counteract unhealthy influences in a pupil's early childhood. They have the power to affect a child's life for better or for worse. A child becomes what he experiences. While parents possess the original key to their offspring's experience, teachers have a spare key. They too can open or close the minds and hearts of children.

In this chapter college students remember their elementary and high school teachers. They recall their images and assess their impact.

"HOW IS THE VACUUM OF YOUR MIND?"

"Our English teacher had a unique talent for complicating life. After an explanation of his, even a simple subject sounded complex. His main interest was in logistics: tests taken on time, papers typed properly, homework handed in promptly. The psychology of teaching and learning escaped him. He took special pains, or perhaps pleasure, to confront us with our bitter reality, as he saw it: 'How is the vacuum of your mind today?' he would ask casually. His corrosive sarcasm painted a bleak picture of our future. 'Soon enough,' he would warn, 'you will knock your head on the ceiling of your ability.' "

THE VALUE OF ZERO

"My arithmetic teacher was crammed with knowledge but he managed to make me feel ignorant. He was extremely erudite but his tongue was a sword. He was a virtuoso of the verbal slap. In his class, we knew how it felt to be a zero."

ECHOES OF EVENTS

"Our history teacher had an indelible impact on my life. Though old, he was contemporary and passionate. He loved life and art. He enjoyed translating the lessons of the past into guidelines for the future. He picked the bones of history delicately, treating its heroes with reverence. A refined and eloquent speaker, he was the epitome of the gentle-man scholar."

THE NAZI

"I attended elementary school in Germany and I have much to forget. But one teacher I shall always remember with special hate. Mr. Eingemacht was like a movie caricature of a Nazi: arrogant, machine-like, and without mercy. Above all, he demanded order. Submissive to the principal, he was a tyrant in the classroom. We had to sit straight and keep our mouths shut. For a minor misdemeanor, he slapped us. For major ones he employed a wooden ruler. I was terrified of him and prayed for his death, but my prayers were never answered. School left a ter-rible mark on my personality: I still expect a repri-manding slap whenever I assert myself."

DRAMA AND LIFE

"Our drama teacher was a true poet and a gen-tle critic. We were an arrogant bunch and thought we knew it all. He could easily have showed up our ignorance. Instead, he captivated our imaginations and captured our hearts. He never criticized, he coaxed. He never pushed, he persuaded. He never insulted, he inspired. With sensitivity he taught us to contrast drama and life, to evaluate performance and character. Through his efforts I came to appreciate art and to choose the theater as my life."

"TIME TO KNOW US"

"My favorite teacher, Mr. Daniel, was a most unforgettable character. He took time to know us. He encouraged us to talk about our lives, about our home and family, our wishes, our fears, our frustrations. In a short time, he knew me better than did my parents. In contrast to my father's brusque manner, Mr. Daniel's approach was mild and engaging. He listened to us, and we had something to say. He rarely raised his voice or used harsh words. He never attacked; he pointed out what needed to be done and stood by ready to give help."

CONCISE CONTEMPT

"As long as I live I'll loathe my English teacher. He was the meanest man I knew before I was ten. He was a master of the double insult:

" 'Stupid idiot!'

" 'Silly fool!'

" 'Dumb blockhead!'

"Like a rattlesnake, he always had fresh venom. He used to tell us that in his mind he had a picture of a perfect pupil. Compared to this brainchild, we were a dismal disappointment. We were 'ignorant illiterates' wasting professional time and public money. His relentless diatribes undercut our self-respect and ignited our hatred. When he finally fell ill, the whole class celebrated in Thanksgiving."

THE CORE TRUTH

"We were the luckiest class in school. We had a homeroom teacher who knew the core truth of education: 'Self-hate destroys, self-esteem saves.' This principle guided all her efforts on our behalf. She always minimized our deficiencies, neutralized our rage, and enhanced our natural gifts. She never, so to speak, forced a dancer to sing or a singer to dance. She allowed each of us to light his own lamp. We loved her, but the school board thought her dangerous. She defied too many official orthodoxies. She did not use tests and grades, and she was against punishment. She did not believe that academic achievement necessarily leads to individual fulfillment, or even to financial success. I remember one of her favorite anecdotes:

"Brown and Green met after an interval of twenty years. Brown was surprised to see Green so rich and prosperous, for he had been such a backward student in school. 'How did you fare so well?' asked Brown. 'Well,' answered Green, 'I knew I wasn't so smart as the rest of you, so I looked for a simple business. I found a product I could make for one dollar and sell for five, and, believe me, over the years, these *four percents really add up.'*

"We got the point and saw hope—even if we were not geniuses."

OVERCONCERN

"Our homeroom teacher approached us with fidgety delicacy. She created around us an air of fragility, as though we were in constant danger of falling apart. She dramatized little hurts and alarmed us with her excessive caution. Her hysterical concern for our welfare made us uneasy. We sensed her despair, her need for our love, and her lack of security. She made us feel responsible for her happiness and guilty for her misery."

TRUST

"One teacher I'll never forget. He helped me to change my view of myself and the world. Until I met him, I had a gruesome picture of grownups. I had no father and my mother was working. My grandpa was grumpy and my grandma angry. She argued and accused, and he bullied and blamed. My first teacher was a mean woman, a copy of my grandma. She, too, provoked and punished. My other teachers were indifferent. As long as I was silent, they were satisfied. If I dropped dead quietly, they wouldn't have minded. I was none of their business.

"Then I met Mr. Benjamin, my sixth-grade teacher. He was different. He delighted in our company. In his presence, we felt important; what we thought made a difference. He believed in us and guided us, appealing to our pride and imagination. 'The world needs your talents,' he would assure us. 'There is suffering and sickness and slums. You can be your brother's keeper or his killer. You can bring hell or help. You are each other's agents of agony or of comfort. In every situation, you can become part of the solution, or part of the problem.' His words still ring true in my heart and affect my life for the better."

LESSONS IN FILIBUSTER

"Our civilization teacher believed in reasoning and he bored us to death. He wasted his energy trying to convince us that we were wrong and stupid. So we hit back with sharp tongues. In his eyes he was a liberal teacher; but in fact, he turned the class into a debating society. We learned little except baiting and arguing. While he celebrated the triumph of the democratic process, we learned the art of filibuster."

LESSONS IN INDIFFERENCE

"Miss G. was the most irrelevant teacher I remember. Her world was the classroom, her desk the center of her universe. From it she ruled compulsively, unleashing her misery on our young minds. Her lectures were the self-revelations of a tormented soul. Having plenty of time and a captive audience, she talked endlessly.

"In the beginning we felt her fury. Then we tired of it and let her boil without notice. We became deaf to her thunder and blind to her anguish. She cried, and we played."

"HURRY SLOWLY"

"In contrast to other teachers Mrs. Sullivan seldom talked about the future. She focused on making the present pleasant. She rarely rushed us: 'Hurry slowly,' she would quip. She was interested not only in our homework, but also in our home lives. She was not afraid to mind our business. She knew how frustrating parents can be, and she often pleaded our case before them, obtaining for us greater autonomy."

"TOO GOOD FOR THE COMMON PEOPLE"

"What angered me most about our French teacher was his partiality toward some students. He had different laws for rich and poor, powerful and meek. Physical punishment was reserved for the weak and defenseless. The rich children were never smacked; he treated them with deference. It was obvious that he feared their parents. The poor had no such protection. In his eyes we were white trash, undeserving of common courtesy. He resented having to teach us. He was too good for the common people."

A SENSE OF MYSTERY

"Our art teacher, Mr. Greco, was a painter with a poetic soul. Mystical and idiosyncratic in his art, he was real and direct in life. We thrived on this vital contrast. Most teachers warned us to face reality; Mr. Greco endowed us with a sense of mystery. Tragedy and joy were personal acquaintances of his. A refugee, he had known sorrow. Suffering brought him wisdom, which he imparted with grace and nobility."

HARVEST OF HATE

"Our health education teacher, Mr. H., saw it as his duty to humble our spirits. Mr. H. worked hard to prove to us that we were incompetent. Keen-eyed, he saw all our faults. In a crisp and cold voice he would tell us what we lacked. And he knew our flaws by heart: We lacked intelligence, manners, character, grace. We were dumb and corrupt and beyond salvation.

"In his class we developed a sense of the ridiculous, an ear for platitudes and an eye for the grotesque. We also learned to defend ourselves against adult attack. We grew indifferent to teacher talk as one does to the clacking of a touch typist.

PROGRAMMED ROBOT

"I have always been slow with numbers. But my math teacher treated me as though I were a wrongly programmed robot whose wires she had to change. I had nothing to say about this operation. No one asked me how I felt about the projects invented for me. I was tutored mercilessly. I was pushed, tested, and retested. My teacher was determined to prove that no one in her class could fail. But I succeeded in surprising her."

A MAGIC TOUCH

"Our history teacher had a magic touch. His classes set our minds on fire. We emerged from them as if from a dream. He understood our longing for adventure and led us into a labyrinth of legends, myths, and mysteries. He was funny in his imitation of historic figures; each era was evoked vividly. His lectures were lucid; the specific and the symbolic emerged with clarity. One lesson he drove home: Historical truth is never final. It is discovered, forgotten, and must be rediscovered endlessly."

MAGNETIC FIELDS

"To our science teacher we were magnetic fields that he could manipulate to make patterns of his own design. We were things to turn, objects to fling. He played our emotions as though they were iron filings. He pulled and stretched and sprinkled them for his own peculiar pleasures. His grotesque humor entertained him. We hurt and hated."

NO EXIT

"Miss C., our homeroom teacher, looked at our class as her private property. Our deportment and scholarship touched directly on her personal prestige. So she taught with a vengeance. She was moralistic and puritanical. A grammatical error would arouse her ire. A common four-letter word sent her into hysterics. We sensed that she was sick, but no one listened to our complaints until the day she was hospitalized. One morning, in a fit of rage, she walked out of our class, using the nearest exit—a third-floor window."

GOLDEN TONGUE

"Mr. King was our favorite teacher, and we were his favorite class. He confessed that he never had a 'collection' quite like us. His English hour was the best part of our day. Mr. King had two outstanding qualities: genuine warmth and a golden tongue. He brought to life the heroes of history and the lions of literature. In his presence we talked fluently. No one stammered in his class. We spoke our minds boldly. Some teachers made us feel guilty and evil when we revealed our thoughts. Not Mr. King. The affection in his eyes gave assurance and dissolved fear. He provided us with incandescent moments that I still treasure."

AN AUTOBIOGRAPHY

"Our Social Studies teacher was a master of the irrelevant monologue. She tried hard to feign an air of mysticism and to convey the agony of the struggling scholar. But she managed only to engender contempt. Her lessons were thickly embroidered with personal case history. We heard a great deal about her mother and father and crazy sister. But we learned little about Social Studies. The whole course was an autobiographical journey—a metaphor for herself."

REVERENCE FOR LIFE

"Our biology teacher was a most memorable man. He was a scientist whose credo was 'Scientific progress *not* at the expense of humanity.' His reverence for life radiated into his daily dealings with students. His lessons were a delight—he was fresh and funny and devoid of sarcasm. He was the dramatic opposite of the antiseptic teacher who preached peace in the world while creating dissension in the classroom."

VERBAL PARSIMONY

"The class came alive the moment Mrs. Cantor entered the room. She brought an intensity to her teaching. She infected us with curiosity and vitality. Even those who resisted her at first slowly came under her spell. She was direct and transparent. Her responses never muddled our mind. Her answers were clear, even when she made us question our basic beliefs. She was a master of verbal parsimony. She made a statement and resisted embellishment."

AT HOME IN THE WORLD

"Mr. Jacobs won our hearts, because he treated us as though we were already what we could only hope to become. Through his eyes we saw ourselves as capable and decent and destined for greatness. He gave direction to our longings and left us with the conviction that our fate can be forged by our hopes and deeds; that our lives need not be shaped by accident; that our happiness does not depend upon happenstance. Mr. Jacobs introduced us to ourselves. We learned who we were and what we wanted to be. No longer strangers to ourselves, we felt at home in the world.

A POEM TO A TEACHER
By M. G.

I cannot write poetry, yet how else
    can I tell.
How tell of this man among men—
    not tall, not fair;
Bringing no gifts, speaking no harsh
    words.
How tell of the miracle he wrought:
    the loosening of the cords binding
    my soul, the cutting of the
    strings which draw tight the
    shutters of my mind.
How else can I tell you of his
    listening heart.

❈ EPILOGUE

On the first day of the new school year, all the teachers in one private school received the following note from their principal·

> Dear Teacher:
> I am a survivor of a concentration camp. My eyes saw what no man should witness:
> Gas chambers built by *learned* engineers.
> Children poisoned by *educated* physicians.
> Infants killed by *trained* nurses.
> Women and babies shot and burned by *high school* and *college* graduates.
> So, I am suspicious of education.
> My request is: Help your students become human. Your efforts must never produce learned monsters, skilled psychopaths, educated Eichmanns.
> Reading, writing, arithmetic are important only if they serve to make our children more humane.

✿ A SELECTED
BIBLIOGRAPHY

COMBS, A. W., AVILA, D. L., AND PURLEY, W. W. *Helping Relationships*. Boston: Allyn and Bacon, 1971.

GINOTT, H. G. *Group Psychotherapy with Children*. New York: The McGraw-Hill Book Co., 1961.

GINOTT, H. G. *Between Parent and Child*. New York: The Macmillan Company, 1965.

GINOTT, H. G. *Between Parent and Teenager*. New York: The Macmillan Company, 1969.

GROSS, BEATRICE, AND GROSS, R., Eds. *Radical School Reform*. New York: Simon and Schuster, 1969.

HENRY, J. *Culture against Man*. New York: Random House, 1963.

HOLT, J. *The Underachieving School*. New York: Delta, 1969.

KOUNIN, J. S. *Discipline and Group Management in Classrooms*. New York: Holt, Rinehart and Winston, 1970.

PINES, MAYA. *Revolution in Learning*. New York: Harper and Row, Publishers, 1966.

RATHS, L. E., HARMIN, M., AND SIMON, S. B. *Values and Teaching*. Columbus, Ohio: Charles E. Merrill Publishing Company, 1966.

REDL, F. *When We Deal with Children*. New York: The Free Press, 1966.

SILBERMAN, C. E. *Crisis in the Classroom*. New York: Random House, 1970.

❋ INDEX